Praise for *Sex on the First Date*
Tim and Kathy Bush

Fiery passion, fearless leadership, fierce commitment, financial prominence. Without a relationship with the One who gave them, those gifts brought Tim and Kathy heartache and pain. Then they met the Giver. Now, He's using those gifts, purified, to bless thousands. It has been my great privilege to watch their transformation and growing ministry. This book shares their amazing story. To Him be the glory!

—**Dave Bechtel, Senior Pastor, New Heights Church, Richland, WA**

Our marriage can be our legacy. We are so moved and inspired by the stories and wisdom throughout this book! The fact that our healthy marriage can be a lasting legacy and proof of the gospel for our children, grandchildren, and generations to come, is so powerfully put on display within these pages. Tim and Kathy have captured our hearts with their boldness, vulnerability, and humility as they let their personal and powerful story be known to a lost and broken world. We dare you read this and to put what you have learned into practice!

—**Justin and Falon Unger, Founders of Likewise Worship**

Real, raw, and vulnerable. We are grateful for the Bushes' honesty about their struggle to find God and each other. God has redeemed their mess and will use it to encourage you.

—**Ron and Nan Deal, Marriage Authors and Speakers**

For any couple who needs just a sliver of hope to stick together, share a few moments with our friends Tim and Kathy. As you ride the ups and mostly downs of their marriage, you'll wonder, Could this get any worse?! But before they could run out on each other, they discovered a Redeemer who was running harder after them—and as you encounter their refreshingly honest story, you might just hear His footsteps coming after you.

—**Brian and Jennifer Goins, Speakers with *Weekend to Remember* and FamilyLife Ministries**

Tim and Kathy tell their story with honesty and hope. Few couples experience the kind of marital pain and heartache that they have, but every marriage can embrace the hope of Jesus that changed the Bushes' lives and saved their marriage. No matter the depths of your despair, their story is a reminder to us all: "But where sin increased, grace increased all the more."

—**Dr. Phillip and Jamie Dunn, Senior Pastor,**
First Baptist Church, Mt. Juliet, TN

Tim and Kathy Bush are living proof that no matter how dead you think your marriage is, God specializes in resurrection! He knows how to bring beauty from ashes. Their story will encourage you and bring you hope, no matter where you are.

—**Bob Lepine, Author of *Love Like You Mean It***
and former Cohost of *FamilyLife Today*

Sex on the First Date paints a realistic picture of how Satan seduces us into falsely believing the web of lies—that people (and things) will satisfy our every fantasy. If you have ever struggled in your marriage, felt as if you have lost all hope, or felt isolated and wonder if it was worth staying even one more day, you will be inspired by Tim and Kathy's story. Their story will infuse every couple with a newfound hope. The Bushes invite you to put a stake in the ground. Will you? This book is a must-read for every person who has walked the road of bringing two imperfect humans together and has a deep desire to live out God's beautiful design for marriage.

—**Debbie Rasa, Executive Director of Life Unplugged,**
Business Partner in Rasa Floors LP and Coaching
| Consulting LLC, and Multi-Jet Rated Pilot

A crazy romance drama . . . only it's a true story! Tim and Kathy's story will pull you in from the first page. From a pattern of the worst imaginable betrayals and hopelessness to the most wonderful, trusting, God-filled union, this book will be a catalyst to saving many marriages, and it offers hope of complete redemption, not only to your marriage, but your life as well.

—**Greg and Julie Gorman, Founders**
of Married for a Purpose

SEX
ON THE
FIRST
DATE

A Story of a Broken Beginning
to a Radically Transformed Marriage

BY TIM AND KATHY BUSH
WITH LISA STILWELL

Forefront
BOOKS

Published by Forefront Books, Nashville, Tennessee.
Distributed by Simon & Schuster.

Library of Congress Control Number: 2023919106

Print ISBN: 978-1-63763-271-0
E-book ISBN: 978-1-63763-272-7

Cover Design by Faceout Studio, Molly von Borstel
Interior Design by PerfecType, Nashville, TN
Printed in the United States of America

DEDICATION

To all the married and thinking-about-getting-married couples who will use our story as a tool to strengthen their marriages.

And to our children, their spouses, and all of our grandchildren who know Granny and Papa as new creations. May our legacy continue through you.

CONTENTS

PART ONE

FOREWORD

By Dennis and Barbara Rainey

Stories of overcoming impossible odds are always heart-warming. They can also be showstoppers. On social media, posts of good news can generate tens of thousands of likes. But the good news is Tim and Kathy's beyond-belief story prompts so much more than clicking a heart and moving on.

In this book you will meet two people very much like yourself. Though their life choices may not match yours, their hearts and their hopes are no different than yours. And the wonder of their miraculous redemption will inspire you to believe God for the same in your own life.

This is a very real read with twists and turns that will probably shock you. Lies, betrayal, drugs, and alcohol all factor large in the drama of their lives. Barbara and I have known Tim and Kathy since 2014, but as we read their book and learned the details of their lives, we marveled in every chapter that they didn't blow up in a puff of smoke, that they didn't both quit, or even worse, murder each other. It's been our experience after working with couples for over fifty years that very few survive such habitual and cyclical deceit and betrayal.

Sex on the First Date is no soap opera fiction. In many ways, it's a Cinderella story of hopelessness reborn to vibrant hope. As you read, you will experience a taste of their release from prison to freedom, their once being blind to finally seeing, and their once living by lies to, today, living by truth.

Tim and Kathy know the reality of resurrection in the here and now. And I can promise you, you will *repeatedly* marvel at the story you are about to read.

Tim and Kathy's marriage was a *very* real mess. Dead. The reason they were able to get back up again and again is because God showed up, and they chose to believe Him when He said, "Follow Me." Their journey shows how His power to work miracles is most obvious in a graveyard.

Today God is using them and their story to bring the message of hope and redemption to thousands of other couples, one home at a time.

Whether you have a strong marriage that you want to invest in, a marriage that needs a jump start, or one that is a *very* real mess, we predict that this book is going to be a page turner.

Their story is not unlike what's happening in your neighborhood, place of work, or even your church. Those folks need the help and hope that the Bushes provide.

So, buy this book . . . no wait, buy two of them! You will likely run into many in your sphere of influence who need solid encouragement. Tim and Kathy deliver!

INTRODUCTION

By Dave and Ann Wilson

I will never forget the day Ann and I met Tim and Kathy. We met on the Family Life "Love Like You Mean It" marriage cruise. Ann and I gave a talk on God's design for married sex and were then required to sign autographs in a room with all the other main stage speakers. That was a joke to us because we were not nationally known authors and speakers like the other presenters, so we knew that no one would come for our autograph. And we were right. Everyone walked right past our table to get the autographs of the other known personalities. Little did we know then, but our lives were about to change.

Tim and Kathy walked up to us and said, "We don't want your autograph, we want you to come to Washington state and do a marriage conference at our church." Tim didn't really present this as a question. It was more of a "You two are coming to our church, and God is going to transform our region." We soon discovered that our friendship with Tim and Kathy would be life changing for both of us as couples.

We have spoken at marriage conferences all over the country for the last thirty-plus years, but this one would mark us forever. Tim and Kathy picked us up at the airport and drove straight to the church where they said their prayer team was waiting. We quickly discovered that this was not a few couples, but a prayer army that was believing God for miraculous transformations of marriages and legacies. Tim and Kathy are two of the strongest spiritual leaders that Ann and I have ever met. They had developed an army of couples who want to see God move big time in bringing Jesus back to the center of the home. And we got to see just that happen.

Over the next ten years, we have done life and ministry with Tim and Kathy, and God heals marriages everywhere they go. Their story is one of the most raw and real and powerful examples of what Jesus can do in and through a couple who totally surrenders to Him. As we read the book that you are now holding, we just wept at what God has done in them and pray that you too will choose to let Jesus do the same in you. The miracle that God did, and is still doing, in Tim and Kathy, He can do in your marriage as well. This book will show you how.

One of the great moments in our life was meeting Tim and Kathy. We are praying that as you meet them in the pages of this book that you will be marked like we have and that you will join Tim and Kathy in allowing God to use you, like them, to transform marriages and families all over this world.

Dear Readers,

This book is based on our true-life story. Some of what we say is our best recollection; all things we share are as we remember. Our hope is that our story gives you hope in whatever place you are in your marriage relationship. Hopefully, from reading our story, you can see that any marriage is salvageable.

PART ONE

1

Caught!

Marriage . . . I'd say it can be one of the most exciting experiences two people can have in life, yet at the same time be one of the most challenging—and my marriage to Kathy was no different. We definitely had some good times, or so I thought, but there were undeniably some valleys that caused us either to search for help that would "fix" us or clinch the thought of ending things once and for all. This day was when I did just that—I had had enough . . .

As I woke up and got ready for work, I couldn't help but feel somewhat proud. The 3,500-square-foot condo we'd built on the Columbia River was a far cry from the duplex Kathy and I rented together on the air force base twenty-four years before. We were so poor then, we had to use hot air from the dryer vent to stay warm. But this condo was custom-built with every amenity Kathy asked for, and I was feeling good and proud of myself and my success. I was also feeling good about Kathy and me. We had a great morning of sex together, and my thoughts quickly got busy thinking about the rounds I would make at my car dealership and commercial construction sites. I like to catch up on the latest from my managers by engaging with them and all the other employees as well. It was going to be a good day.

I said bye to Kathy as I walked by her home office overlooking the river and headed out the door into the garage. I started my car and began to back out, but then I got a quick rush of wanting to kiss her goodbye, so I decided to go back inside. As I went in, I heard her on the phone, so I stood very quietly and listened. Her tone caught my attention because she sounded so warm—she was not talking to her mom or sister or any other woman. Then I heard the words, "Things aren't going well in my marriage. How are things going with yours? . . . I really miss talking to you." It became more and more clear she was talking to a man, and I figured out it was a guy she'd had an affair with a few years before, only I thought it was over.

Apparently *not*.

My heart raced and quickly took a dive—I felt *crushed*—and I thought, *Here we go again . . .* It'd only been five minutes since I said goodbye to her, thinking everything was fine, and she'd wasted no time trying to rekindle an old relationship.

When Kathy finally saw me, she froze with a complete look of guilt on her face, then quickly said, "I have to go," and hung up.

I could tell she knew she'd been caught. There was *no* denying. As she looked down at a card on her desk, I walked over and reached for it and said, "What's this?"

"A phone card . . ."

"Well, I'm going to trace every call you've made on this!"

Kathy sank. She knew she was caught even more. The call she made that morning was one of many she'd made while she had recently been away at school, and I would expose them all.

For the first time, I wanted a divorce.

And for the first time, Kathy didn't.

She had confessed only weeks before after returning from an eight-month aesthetics school that she slipped into several indiscretions, but she was sorry and would do whatever she could to make things work with us. I believed her. And that morning I thought everything was back under control, and controlling things was something I worked hard at doing. As long as she was under control, I felt okay, but at that moment, I could feel the stresses that come with realizing my sense of control was only in my mind and not a reality.

Kathy *begged* me to give her another chance. She agreed that we were at a final crossroads considering everything we'd been through, and she would do everything possible to make it work. She even suggested a husband-and-wife counseling team we could go to and that she'd make the first appointment they had available.

I agreed, but deep down, I felt unsettled. Not only because of what had just happened, but because of my own dark secrets I'd kept inside, it was the only short season in our marriage I'd actually been faithful to Kathy . . . and now I thought God was getting back at me. I didn't know God then, but I did believe there was a God and that He was letting my promiscuity come back to haunt me. But even if this were the case, I would never tell. I'd keep Kathy in her place and my actions would stay locked away inside of me. I had been told these are things you take to your grave. I would *never* give full disclosure.

———————

I remember that day and the state of mind I was in very well, and it wasn't framed with the same "It's going to be a good day" Tim felt. And I certainly didn't have a great morning of sex—I was left feeling empty, as usual. Looking back, it was the beginning of another cycle, where he and I would be doing well, then I would begin to feel alone and long for something that was missing. I was searching to find myself. This usually started with alcohol and sometimes involved another man, then eventually confessing to Tim what I'd done, receiving his so-called forgiveness, then falling right back into the way our marriage had always been: Tim being in control. Since we first got married, Tim controlled everything—my role as a wife and mother, when we had sex, and, of course, the money. He wouldn't even let me do the grocery shopping early in the marriage—he had to do that too.

I'll never forget the first time Tim "let" me go to the grocery store by myself. I was twenty-one years old, we'd been married three years and had three kids, and I wanted to plan the meals and do the grocery shopping. So Tim gave me the checkbook, and off I went in our Ford Ranchero. I felt excited and wanted everything to go perfectly. I spent two hours getting everything on the list and checking the prices. As I paid, a guy bagged them and then helped me load them into the back of my truck. Then I noticed right next door was a Payless drugstore, so I quickly walked over to pick up my birth control pills. I wasn't in the store more than five minutes before I walked back to my car and found that all of the groceries were gone! Someone took all the groceries! I was crushed.

I started crying and kept crying while I drove home thinking I would be in so much trouble with Tim. In my mind, we had more of a father/daughter relationship because of how he controlled the marriage. Fortunately, Tim wasn't upset. In fact, he consoled me and encouraged me to go back, but I couldn't do it. I felt as though I had failed.

Being controlled and not getting the emotional connection I needed, I began to turn to other men for love and for someone who would really listen to me. I felt excitement and acceptance from them. After twenty-four years of trying, I had accepted the fact that my marriage wouldn't be all that I wanted, so I'd do the best I could and on occasion have an affair to fill the void Tim left.

That morning, a guy I had had an affair with came to mind, and I felt drawn to reach out to talk to him and rekindle anything that might be there. So as soon as Tim walked out of the house, I dialed his number and was literally on the phone with him while standing at the window from my office to watch Tim's car back out. Only it never did. And by the time I realized he hadn't left, I turned and saw him in the doorway listening. Before that incident, I had gone to Tim to confess what I'd done out of guilt and remorse, but this time, he caught me right in the act.

In Case You Were Wondering . . .
KATHY

What was going through my head as I picked up the phone and called another man just days after confessing to Tim what I had done in school and then just after having sex with him that morning . . . I wasn't thinking. I was so selfish, living in the moment in an empty marriage and trying to fill the void with either someone or something else to make me happy. I had decided I would settle for our marriage the way it was and believed that if I wanted anything more, I would have to go outside of it, even though during and after every act of infidelity, I felt anything but satisfied. I knew I was wrong, but I also felt like I deserved to be happy and that's what it would take.

It was a pivotal point in our marriage because we both knew we just couldn't keep going the way we had for so many years. The kids were grown and gone, and we either had to figure out how to be married—meaning without infidelity—or get a divorce. Tim had previously told me about two affairs he'd had, but as far as I knew, I was the one who'd created most of the situation because mine were more numerous and consistent with our cycle. Whenever we'd gone to counseling, it was always to fix me. So at that point, I was willing to get some specialized counseling together.

In Case You Were Wondering . . .
TIM

What I thought when I heard Kathy talking on the phone . . . in my mind, this phone call was God getting back at me for all my indiscretions, which Kathy knew nothing about.

Little did I know of the extent of Tim's unfaithfulness and the measures he took to hide it. But before going there, I think it's important to step back and look at the bigger picture, such as why and how we ended up there in the first place; why and how does any marriage end up at such a crossroads? Why couldn't our *marriage be satisfying enough to keep and hold us in our commit-ment we had made almost a quarter-century earlier?*

I think some of the answers are that marriage doesn't nec-essarily begin on a wedding day—it begins with the upbringings and backgrounds that lead two people toward each other. And both Tim's and my upbringings were catalysts for marrying for all the wrong reasons yet staying for all the right ones . . .

WHAT ABOUT YOU?

As Tim said, marriage can be one of the most challenging rela-tionships two people will ever experience. It's natural to look to each other to be the source for filling your emotional and phys-ical needs, but no one can meet all of their spouse's needs—it's just not possible. So when we have that expectation and they fail, disappointment sets in, and the temptation to look to someone or something else is very real. I know firsthand that having an affair isn't the answer. Oh, it feels that way at first, but each time, I found myself dealing with the same void I felt with Tim in each boyfriend I found, and it took a while to figure that out. It's vital to keep searching and working together as a husband and wife rather than giving in to despair and "settling" for whatever else you think is the answer. It's also vital not to have deceit or secrets from or between each other. Only truth will bring healing, even when the truth hurts.

It's also difficult to live with someone who tries to con-trol you—or if you are controlling toward them. In my case, I was overbearing and made it difficult for Kathy to grow into the woman she longed to be. Her potential and confidence weren't allowed to surface, and she suffered for a long time with yielding to discouragement and giving in to whatever I told her to do. She wanted a voice, and I didn't allow room for her to express it.

Remember: The problems we all face within marriage are fixable as long as commitment remains. Ideally, both husband and wife would hold on together. In our case, at least one of us didn't want out when the other did, which kept us together. Either way, working through challenges takes patience and at the very least, a continual determination not to give up.

QUESTIONS FOR TRANSFORMATION———

- Is there anyone in your life who tempts you to believe they will offer you more than your spouse can? Are you tempted to act inappropriately outside of your marriage covenant? Are you willing to take the steps needed to create distance from him or her and press into your spouse instead?

- Are there any ways you try to control your spouse instead of allowing her or him to be themselves? Do you allow the freedom, even encouragement they need to be their own person and develop their gifts and talents?

2

How We Began:
Tim's Story

I think Kathy is right when she says our upbringings play an important part of who we are as adults and how we interact with others, especially a spouse. You can look at behavior now and trace it back to how and why it developed from an early age. For me, I can look back on certain things I definitely carried into marriage that I'm not proud of, yet no child has control over what happens to them in regard to the authority figures they look to and rely on, and my childhood was no exception.

For starters, my mother, Janett, married nine times to seven different men. Yes, that's right, *nine* times to *seven* men. I was born from her first marriage to George Steinauer, which only lasted about a year. Then she married my little brother's dad, Bill, who physically abused me. I'm talking beating-to-the-point-of-putting-me-in-the-hospital level of abuse. I watched him beat my mom too. I remember my grandmother, Gram, threatening to kill him for what he did. So my mom divorced him.

On a side note, it actually took me over forty years to get counseling and work through those memories and come to a point of forgiving him. I didn't yet know the full concept of forgiveness, but there was something about letting go that I knew I needed to do. When I realized this, my brother, Ned, had been in hospice dying from brain cancer. I wanted Ned to witness me granting Bill forgiveness before Ned died. That Saturday morning, filled with anxiety, I was standing on one side of the bed and Bill was standing on the other. He was a seventy-year-old broken man by then with his only son dying in front of him.

I looked at him and said, "I want you to know, Bill, I forgive you for what you did to me as a kid." I don't recall what he said in response—the exchange was so surreal to me; all I remember is Ned died shortly after that, and I felt better for forgiving Bill.

In Case You Were Wondering...
TIM

Why I carried a burden of bitterness for Ned's dad for over forty years . . . carrying it was part of my survival. It made me feel like I was in control, but I wasn't. Not granting forgiveness hurt me more than it helped. Unforgiveness can be toxic, even to the point of hurting other relationships not involved in the original offense. I learn and will share much more later about forgiveness.

Well, after my mom divorced him, she married Herman. I was about seven or eight. I remember Herman went to a

Baptist church and thought I needed to get baptized, so I did, even though I didn't know what I was doing. That was the only form of church I had experienced to that point.

Mom and Herman were only married about seven months, but during that time, I watched him beat her too. One time I walked into the kitchen to see him beating her, and I grabbed an iron skillet off the stove, hit him over the head, and knocked him out cold. We lived in a mobile home on my grandparents' farm, so I ran to their house, burst in, and said, "I killed Herman! I *killed* him!" I literally thought I'd killed him. So Gram and Pop went over to our house to find that he wasn't dead. I didn't kill him after all, and I'm relieved to this day I didn't have to live with the thought if I had. Soon after, my mom divorced him.

The next guy she married was Bob, and he physically abused me too, but he was also emotionally abusive. I was about eight or nine, and it's hard to talk about to this day, but one of the things I remember is going on a trip to Yellowstone National Park. We rode in a two-door yellow Dodge Dart with Bob and my mom in the front seat, and Bob's two kids and my brother and me in the back with two dogs. When we stopped at restaurants for dinner, Mom and Bob would order steak, and each of us kids would get a dollar, which would be enough for a bowl of soup, lots of crackers, and water.

Well, I had a lot of stomach issues by then and suffered from diarrhea, so I had to go to the bathroom a lot. I think it was from always eating soup and crackers, along with the stress I was under. One time after leaving a restaurant, we were driving through the park, and everyone kept talking about all the bears that were out there. When it was about to get dark, I had to go to the bathroom, but there were no bathrooms anywhere. Bob stopped the car and said, "You can hold it or you can get out now, and we're not waiting. We're leaving." I didn't know what else to do other than get out of the car so I could go the bathroom, so I did, and off he drove. There I was, standing by myself feeling completely abandoned in Yellowstone, absolutely scared I was going to get mauled by a bear. I remember seeing Ned looking at me with tears streaming down his face as they drove away. He was about four years old.

After what seemed like twenty minutes, Bob finally came back to get me, and my little brother was still crying pretty hard, so you can imagine the emotional trauma this put him through too.

I remember at one point while living with Bob, my Gram shoved a dime in a hole in my tennis shoe and told me that when things got too rough, to call her. And I did a couple of times—even collect—when I got scared.

Eventually my mom divorced Bob, and there were other husbands after this. At one point she met a guy that wanted to marry her, but he wouldn't because she had kids—and he didn't want kids. So she went to my brother's dad and told him she couldn't handle having kids anymore and asked him to take Ned. Bill agreed. Then she went to her parents—my grandparents on the farm—and asked if they would take me.

Well, my Pop was a smart dude and said, "Yeah, we'll take him, but not temporarily. We want to adopt him." She agreed, but he'd have to call my dad to get his permission. Pop brought me to the round kitchen table and sat me down. He wanted me to hear on the rotary phone the conversation he was about to make because he knew it would be profound at some point in my life.

He picked up the phone and called my dad—whom I had only seen a handful of times in twelve years—and said, "Butch, this is Myrl. I'm calling you because Janett wants to give Tim up for adoption; for us to do that, we need your permission."

There was a pause and then Pop said, "No, you don't have to pay the fifty bucks a month anymore."

There was another pause.

Then he said, "Okay, I'll send over all the paperwork. Once you sign and send it back, you'll be relieved of any of your obligations." And he hung up.

As soon as my dad signed the paperwork, my grandparents took me to the local courthouse where we stood in front of a judge, and he said to me, "Tim, this is your opportunity to have any last name you want." And I said, "Well . . . could it be Bush?" It was the only name that held any stable family association for me, so that's what I chose.

I looked at Gram and Pop to see what they thought, and they said, "We were hoping you'd say Bush!" And my life took a drastic turn as I went on to live with them.

―――――――――

By the time I became a Bush, I was in sixth grade, about five feet three inches tall, and weighed about 200 pounds. I was picked on by a lot of kids at school for being very fat. I know those are things kids do, but it hurt! So right away, Gram started feeding me healthy meals of fresh vegetables and meat off the farm. Pop had a lot of foot issues from serving in WWII; even so, he'd put on his oxfords and run with me early mornings. I slowly began to lose weight, get into better shape, and become more popular in school.

At the same time, Pop taught me how to work doing all sorts of things on the farm and other places. He gave me a piece of land to grow corn or whatever I wanted, plus he said I could pick anything on the farm, sell it, and share in the profits. Before long, I had odd jobs all over the neighborhood. I mowed lawns and mucked barns; I'd tear down old barns and sell the wood; and at the age of twelve, I had over five hundred dollars in the bank. Pop really helped set a foundation for a hard work ethic, saving, and investing so I'd be a success . . . especially with women. He always said that if I wanted to have women, I'd need to have money. That didn't mean as much to me at first, but by the time I was fourteen, I started to like girls—and they liked me.

Just before I turned fifteen, I had sex for the first time, and Pop had a sense about it. One morning he approached me and said, "Hey, I know things are starting to get serious with you and your girlfriend," and he handed me a brown paper bag with a box of Trojans. He told me to use them because he didn't want me to get a girl pregnant. By the time I was sixteen, I'd had sex with several girls, and Pop was my cheerleader. He'd get up in the morning and have breakfast waiting for me and ask how last night went—did I score? At one point, I did get a girl pregnant and paid for an abortion, which to this day is hard to think about. But Pop said that someday I'd be married to someone like my Gram the rest of my life, so I needed to make sure I sowed all my wild oats before that happened. So, while Pop did such a good job growing me up into a man, teaching me to be responsible and work hard and make money, he also instilled the mindset that the more women I had sex with, the happier I'd be, and the harder I worked, the more successful—the two went hand in hand. Since Pop was my role model and I loved him more than any other man, I embraced it for all it was worth.

WHAT ABOUT YOU?

We all have a story, and some of us have hard ones to tell. It can be difficult stepping out of your present circumstances, revisiting your roots. and taking a good look at people and events that have hurt you. Even if you had a good childhood, there can still be wounds and brokenness that linger into the way you view life and respond to situations now, without even realizing it. As I write this today, some fifty-plus years later, I'm still getting emotional.

For me, it was hard facing some of the abuse I experienced, yet I'm so glad I did because it's helped me to heal through forgiveness and to understand why I did some of the things I did as I got older, which you'll read more about later. Not that my struggles as a boy justified my behavior as an adult, but the more understanding I've gained, the more I've been able to allow myself some grace and fully embrace the healing I've wanted and needed to keep those negative memories from controlling who I am today.

I'm also glad I've looked back because there were a lot of good memories that played into the kind of man I've grown to be. My Pop and Gram adopted me into their loving home. Pop instilled in me a strong work ethic, wisdom in handling money, and a survivor mentality, all of which have greatly benefited my life in ways beyond what I ever thought possible. Gram loved and nurtured me with consistency I'd not had before. I imagine you have some good times to remember too, which helps balance out the bad.

If you haven't already, will you take the time to look back on your life, allow yourself to face anything you've written off as "Oh, that's in the past," and take steps toward forgiveness and healing? You may even want to lean on professional assistance—whatever is necessary to help you understand who you are today and embrace yourself and your story with fuller acceptance.

QUESTIONS FOR TRANSFORMATION

- My Pop taught me skills I developed and carried throughout my life for the good. There were also some not-so-good ways he influenced me. Is there anyone who is influencing you now in ways you know deep down are not good? We often become like those we associate with, so will you be intentional about who you spend time with for the good?
- Do you have someone you trust pouring into your life? Who do you think of in that category? Could you ask them to mentor you?
- Something else to consider is, who are you influencing for good? How about for the not-so-good? Will you take an honest assessment and reflect on any changes you might need or want to make? Will you put a stake in the ground today to make these positive changes?

3

How We Began: Kathy's Story

*J*ust *like Tim, I can look back at my childhood and see how certain events and conditions created unhealthy actions into adulthood and, ultimately, into my marriage. When you don't have the capacity to protect yourself in ways you need while growing up, it's natural to drown out your pain and act as though you're fine. The problem is, when you do that, it eventually surfaces in harmful ways that affect the decisions you make and the dynamics of your relationships. For me, my childhood from the outside looked normal enough—and it was for the formative years—but on the inside, things were far from it.*

I was born in Calexico, California, and I really can't remember a lot about the places I lived until my middle school years—only bits and pieces. My dad was an immigration officer, and in order to be promoted or take a transfer, he had to be willing to move as needed, so that's what we did every two or three years. And we never lacked excitement in our home. My mom had one baby after another, seven children in all. I came right in the middle, and I was super shy.

I remember with each move, I'd be excited at first, but then once we got settled, I'd have to make new friends, and that wasn't easy for me. So, needless to say, I didn't have many friends—mainly my siblings were my friends.

Overall, I had a pretty good and traditional home life. My dad worked all day, and my mom stayed home with us kids. Taking care of all the duties of so many kids was a lot, but even so, we always had homemade meals and dessert. During the day my siblings and I played together and attended school, which I never did like because I was so shy. It was hard for me to make friends. On the weekends Dad would pull out games to play with us, or he'd grab his guitar and sing, which I loved. My mom, of course, was usually busy with cleaning and cooking and doing what moms do all day, so it was a nice break for her to have Dad take over with us. I really liked to be by myself and didn't require a lot of attention. Mom told me I was such a good baby that when Dad would get home late at night, they would get me out of my crib and play with me.

Church was very important to my mom, so we'd all go every Sunday to a Lutheran church, and Dad seemed to be good with it too. I didn't mind going, but I had a hard time understanding what any of the rituals and sermons meant. I believed in God, and even believed Jesus died for my sins, but I couldn't get much past that basic belief. I went through confirmation and attended youth group activities. We even celebrated Advent every Christmas and Lent at Easter as a family, but it was all done because that's what you're supposed to do when you're in church. I'd try to understand more about God, but it just didn't penetrate. Sometimes when we went to church, I'd sit down in the pew and think, Okay, I'm really going to listen to the message today, and I would, but nothing made sense to me.

Even though I didn't understand much, I'm thankful for the exposure to God my parents gave me. I didn't know it, but even though I struggled to comprehend what I heard then, seeds were being planted in my heart. It just wasn't until later that they got watered and began to grow.

When we took vacations, we didn't take exotic trips on planes and stay in hotels; we'd go and visit family. We'd all pile into our station wagon and Dad would drive us to Idaho to visit my mom's parents, or to New Mexico to see his family. Mom would pack food for us, or occasionally we would stop at restaurants, and Dad would drive straight through the night while we all slept. I remember waking early in the mornings and he'd still be driving and listening to a staticky talk show to help him stay awake. Even though they weren't big, fancy vacations, I have good memories of being together wherever we went. I didn't feel as though I was missing out on anything compared to what other families did.

As I said, my life looked and felt like normal Middle America in my formative years, but as I got older, and Mom and Dad left us kids alone, things began to feel wrong and disturbing. For example, a family member began expressing inappropriate "play" behavior, then manipulating us not to tell Mom and Dad. Even though those times were supposed to be playtimes, they just felt wrong, but I was too young to understand why and articulate it.

But the most difficult thing that happened was around age twelve when another family member began to molest me. When it started, I was so surprised because I loved this person—I trusted them. Not long after it began, I would feel anxious and scared about what might happen when I went to bed, and when it did, I would just freeze—I didn't feel as if I could say no or tell anyone.

The abuse went on for a while, although I've literally blocked out time spans so I can't even say exactly when it started and ended, but I remember being very depressed from that time on. It was a very hard time. I'd go to bed at night and ask God to put me to sleep and take me to heaven. In fact, I wanted to sleep whenever I could because when I did, I could escape and not have to face my life and the sadness of how I felt.

I don't know why I didn't tell my parents. It wasn't until I was an adult that I finally shared what happened, and it wasn't received very warmly—I quickly realized it was not okay to talk about. Even now, it's not something that's talked about.

In my home I had everything I needed, but if I wanted more, I had to pay for it myself. So I started babysitting at twelve and picked cucumbers in the summer. I worked at a gun range at fifteen, then Arby's. Occasionally I would even steal things I wanted from the store but couldn't afford. Even so, I'm thankful my parents encouraged me to work.

By the time I turned sixteen, I began drinking because when I did, alcohol helped me overcome my severe shyness and low self-esteem. I used to pour a random mixture of alcohol I took from my parents' cabinet into an empty Miracle Whip jar, sneak it out of the house, and meet up with a friend to drink together. I didn't care what it tasted like, I just wanted to get drunk. Sometimes I'd meet with different boys who'd bring alcohol, so I'd get drunk with them. When this happened, I became very promiscuous and slept around—and soon I had boyfriends who gave me the "love" or attention I longed for. There were times when a girlfriend and I would go to a dance club and hook up with guys and have sex with them, so, looking back, I can see that that's when I began to develop a pattern of drinking and having sex—on the flip side, I'd never had sex without drinking alcohol.

Finally, one guy I met actually turned into a relationship that lasted almost two years. I was still in high school when I *thought we might even get married. At one point, I even thought I was pregnant by him, but it turned out to be a false alarm. I had no career aspirations—I wanted to get married and have kids the way my mom had. But when I really thought about marriage to this guy, I remember thinking how unmotivated he was. I felt like I wanted more, so I wasn't sure he'd work out. I wanted to be provided and cared for the way my mother was by my dad. So as much as I thought I loved the guy, I wasn't sure he was the one.*

I know now that my hesitancy to marry him was there for good reason because God had a different plan. I was about to meet a man—a real man—one that, at first glance, I'd know would be up for the task. And meeting him was right around the corner . . .

WHAT ABOUT YOU?

There are differing statistics about childhood abuse. A lot of it is not reported because it's not talked about, but the numbers are still high. I know firsthand how its damaging effects can leave scars for a lifetime. If not addressed, the pain will influence the choices you make and spur destructive behavior, as it did in me by drinking alcohol at an early age and becoming promiscuous. The tendency is not to talk about it, yet it's the best thing a person can do to begin their healing process.

One good thing today that wasn't the case when I was grow-ing up is that there's more access for support than ever before. So if you or someone you know lives with such a painful past, I encourage you to get the help you need. Healing is possible, which is so important for becoming whole, and we all deserve to be whole. For me, I'm thankful I was able to forgive my abuser later in my adult life.

And as Tim noted, I'm thankful for the many good memories I had growing up, between both my mom and dad who loved me, my siblings as friends (since I was so shy), wholesome meals, and family togetherness. Yes, I had a few rough years, but I also had many good ones to look back on.

QUESTIONS FOR TRANSFORMATION————

- When anything adverse happens to us, it can affect us throughout our lives if we let it. Is there a harmful habit you've developed over time as a coping mechanism—such as drinking—that has more control over you than you have over it? Will you consider an honest assessment and modify your behavior if needed?

- If we have a harmful experience in childhood, it's not uncommon to live our entire life with shame or fear without even realizing it. And living with either of those can rob us of joy. Will you have courage to acknowledge any time in your life that's plagued you in such a way and seek help with breaking free into true healing?

4

Sex on the First Date

I was twenty years old and basically had everything a young man could want. I thought I was a borderline *rock star*, having achieved the status and success I had worked so hard to attain. I was making close to six figures and knew more was possible. I owned my own house, I partied, drank, smoked weed, dabbled in drugs, and I had a really nice girlfriend—although I was still on the hunt and I cheated on her all the time. I thought I loved her, but I couldn't seem to be true to her. It was nothing she did—I just wasn't able to give my whole self to one person.

Even so, most of the time I felt like I had my life under control by living exactly the way I wanted to, yet deep down I had begun to think I couldn't live like that forever. In the back of my mind, I sensed that something was still missing—there was something else out there for me—but I didn't know what it was or how to find it. I even started to think that if I found a "good" girl—as in one who went to church—her influence would help me to change. I was interested in one or two good girls, but they saw right through me for the most part, or people who cared about them did. And I say now, thank goodness for those people; they are the guardian angels of the world.

It was at this point that I went to my brother Ned's school, Lewis Junior High, the same one I'd attended, to watch him at a track meet . . . and then I saw her. Immediately I thought, *Wow! She's cute!* I was so intrigued by how she looked. Ned knew who she was because he went to school with her sister. The girl's name was Kathy, and Ned was familiar with her family and knew that they were good, churchgoing people. Ned also knew how I was and said, "Don't even think about going out with her, Tim. She's a nice church girl, and you're not necessarily a good dude—you're not good. She's *way* better than you. I know what you do; I see what you do with your girlfriend now; I see you bring other women to the house. I don't want you to take her out." So I didn't approach her, but my thoughts of finding a really good girl—a church girl— weighed even more on my mind. A girl like her could bring on a big change for me. I had asked other church girls out before, but they'd turned me down. Maybe she wouldn't . . .

Then I saw her again. It was a few weeks later and well into summer break when I went to a party just a few houses down from where she lived. I knew that because Ned had been at her house to see her sister. So when I walked into the party, she, once again, caught my eye. And *boy*, did I want to take her out and get to know her. She seemed so special, I wanted it to be different with her than with all the other girls before.

———

I remember that night too. I was invited to a party up the street by a friend who went to the same high school, so I went to check it out. While I was there, a friend came up and said, "That Tim Bush is trying to hook up with me!" And I said, "Who is Tim Bush?" She pointed to a guy standing at a table, and when I looked at him, I thought: A man! Compared to all the other high school guys, he clearly stood out. He wore dress slacks and a nice dress shirt, and he carried himself with confidence.

I said to my friend, "Do you mean that man over there?" She said, "Yeah! That's Tim Bush," as though I should have known who he was. I didn't. All I knew was that he didn't seem to belong at the party by the way he was dressed—he looked far more mature than the rest of the crowd. He even had facial hair.

He didn't speak to me, but later my sister Heidi started talking about Tim. She went to school with his younger brother, Ned, and she said Tim wanted to take me out. When I said I really wasn't interested, she said, "But listen, Tim's got his own house, he's got cars, and he'd probably spend a lot of money on you." With that, she convinced me to change my mind.

A few weeks later I was out drinking with friends—a girl and two other guys—who knew about Tim and heard he was having a party at his house, so we crashed it.

———

I was having a party at my house, alright—in my rock star pad. It was a nicer place than anyone else's I knew of. I built it with my own two hands—and it thrilled me that Kathy showed up with a few friends. Two of them were guys, but I didn't care; it didn't stop me! I made my way over and right away let her see that I was interested in her. I tried to sell myself as much as possible and said, "Hey, we should go out sometime. We could go out for a nice dinner." She said yes! Then she gave me her number.

I decided that if I could take her out, I'd want to do it right—she was too good not to give my full attention. I'd want things to be different with her than with my current and previous relationships, so I made the break with my girlfriend—I wanted to feel free to be in full-on pursuit. The very next day I called Kathy to set up a date and make plans for dinner and a movie.

Ned, who had made his concerns known, would need to know my intentions were good. So I made it a point to tell him—I *promised* him—I'd be nicer to her than I had been to my last girlfriend. I'd be true to this one. I had a feeling she was as special as Ned had implied, so when I asked Kathy out, I had no intention of sleeping with her, whereas normally I would plan on it with anyone else. Things were going to be different with her.

On Labor Day of 1981, only days before her senior year in high school, I drove up to her house. I was prepared to meet her mom, but her dad? He was a law enforcement officer. I knew he would ask me a lot of questions, so I had to be on my best behavior. And I was right.

I walked into the entryway, held out my hand, looked George in the eyes, and said, "Hi, Mr. Hunter. Your daughter is in good hands with me. I'll take good care of her!" Then I said, "We're going to dinner and a movie, so what time do you want her home?" He said one o'clock. Wow! I thought for a first date, that was pretty late, but I was glad because I knew we would have enough time not to be rushed and still have her home by curfew. So the first impression went well. I liked them, and they seemed to like me.

As the time approached for Tim to pick me up, I remember being nervous because I kept thinking of him as a man, not a high school boy, and this was an "official" date. Up to this point, I had gone out with the one guy for the past two years that I mentioned, and a lot of our time together we drank. There were a couple of other guys, but I wasn't nervous with them because we always drank. Now, there I was getting ready to go out with Tim, and I was sober.

When I walked toward the entryway, he was talking to Mom and Dad about our plans. Then he walked me to his car and opened the door, which I thought was nice—not what I was used to. As he walked around to his side and got in, I thought, Wow, he's kinda good looking! *He had shorts on, so I got a good look at his legs, and they were hairy man legs! I wasn't used to seeing that being around high school boys. I also thought his legs were larger than mine, which I liked. I was self-conscious about my body and thought I had kind of fat legs, but next to his, they looked slim, and that made me feel good.*

———————

Off we went to dinner at Old Towne Pizza in Portland, Oregon, with my fake ID in hand. I ordered a pitcher of beer and quickly realized that Kathy couldn't drink much without it affecting her—she hadn't even finished her first glass before she began to relax and get a little giggly. Of course, I had a high tolerance for alcohol, so I could drink more than her.

When we finished and went out to the car, we were already hanging onto each other. Kathy felt good, smelled good, and looked good, and my words to Ned were quickly fading out of mind. We drove to Vancouver, Washington, to Andresen Drive-In Theatre to watch the movie, and even though I didn't take Kathy out with the intent of having sex, I couldn't help but kick into my usual pattern.

As the movie began, I reached toward the back seat for the red and white Playmate cooler I had filled with Schlitz Malt Liquor and grabbed some weed from my glove box, which was a normal setup for me. After we drank a beer and smoked some pot, that was it—we landed in the back seat where we had sex on the first date.

It definitely wasn't intentional for me. When I'd shaken her dad's hand only hours before, my intent was to take good care of his daughter and not take advantage of her in any way. But as I said, it was my pattern—a pattern that had more control over me than I had over it.

———

My memory of that night isn't quite as clear as Tim's, but I do remember drinking another beer in the car and smoking some weed. Then my memory ends. Looking back, whenever I drank and smoked pot, I wouldn't remember things—my mind just blanked out. The next thing I knew, Tim was taking me home. I knew I would have to check in with Mom, so I pulled myself together so she wouldn't know I had been drinking. I woke up the next morning thinking about what I could remember and how much I liked Tim.

In Case You Were Wondering . . .
KATHY

About my not remembering sex on our first date . . . I want to clarify that I did not pass out. Having sex was totally consensual on my part. Between all the alcohol, the weed, and the amount of time that has passed since that time. In life, I just don't remember much. But I will say, this is not the right way to start a healthy relationship, but this was how it started for us.

———

Well, I *do* remember all that happened, and as the evening moved into early morning, I drove Kathy home and thought, I really, really *like this girl. She's so special. She comes from an exceptional family.* I thought she was *special* and *I wanted her for myself!* After I got home, I sat down in the living room and took a bong hit and drank a beer with my roommate, Brian, and said, *"This is the girl I'm going to marry!"* I felt so good. She was "it" for me.

Needless to say, Kathy and I started talking more on the phone and seeing each other as much as we could. I'd even pick her up from school and bring her to my house to drink and talk. Then one afternoon when she came over, I found out she had never had sex without drinking alcohol. A bit later, she started to kiss me, but I stopped her. I looked at her and said, "Kathy, we're not going to have sex again unless we are sober." I wanted our relationship to be more than just about the sex; I wanted it to be different.

———

Yeah, when Tim said he wouldn't have sex again unless we were both sober, I backed away and thought, Ooh, that's going to be hard. *Then I told him,* "I've never done that, I'm afraid. I don't

think I can, so it's not going to happen now!" And he said, "Well,
that's how it's going to be."

I wasn't expecting him to say that, and I had to process the
thought. Drinking took away my inhibitions, so I wasn't comfort-
able with the idea, yet (even so) as another couple of weeks went
by, we were getting to know a lot more about each other by not
having sex. We probably got to know more in that time than any
other time before we got married.

———

For the next two weeks, we talked on the phone more—
Kathy even got in trouble at times because she hogged the
phone in a house with three other siblings still at home. This
was back when you had one phone the whole family had to
share! We also made it a point not to drink a lot and to be
more intentional about getting to know each other. But that's
about as long as we could last—we couldn't stay away from
each other—and we had sex again. This time, we were sober.

It was also a time when my old girlfriend started calling
me wanting to get back together . . .

WHAT ABOUT YOU?

If you're not married and reading this, you probably understand all too well how real the temptation is to have sex. You
might even be thinking about someone who encourages it,
as was my case. Society in general says it's okay, it's normal.
But looking back, Kathy and I can see how even during those
few weeks, our focus on really getting to know each other
was richer because we weren't having sex. If we could have a
do-over, we'd have waited and spent much more time digging

deeper into learning about each other and talking more about what we each thought marriage looked like, not to mention valuing the sanctity of marriage.

One of the contributing factors as to why we didn't wait was because we drank and smoked weed while we were together, and any inhibitions or efforts not to have sex vanished. We basically sabotaged our chances of keeping our relationship pure.

QUESTIONS FOR TRANSFORMATION————

- For us, drinking definitely affected the decisions we made and our actions toward each other. If you are married and drink alcohol and/or take drugs, how does it affect your everyday interaction with your spouse? How does it affect you when you're not with your spouse? It's good to recognize the signs and do what's best for everyone involved for a marriage that's healthy, strong, and not dependent on a chemical substance.

- If you are married and one of you struggles with drugs or alcohol, are you supporting that spouse in a way that honors them? Supporting your spouse can look different in different relationships. How does your spouse feel about your support? Be honest! (If you're not sure, ask him or her.)

- We will get more into this in chapter 15, but for now: How does alcohol benefit your marriage, if at all?

5

Of Course, I Will Marry You

It had been just a few weeks since going out with Tim, and I was falling real hard. By that I mean my heart was opened in ways I'd not felt before—Tim was so different compared to the younger "boys" I'd been with until then. With them, I had equated sex with love, and even though I often felt used, I thought that's just the way love was. But with Tim, I felt different. We'd spent more time getting to know each other, and then when he insisted we not have sex unless we were both sober, things were very different. I started to fall in love for the first time, and it happened fast. He was all man to me, and I liked it.

I knew he could take care of me, he would protect me, he was responsible, he had a home, plus I felt safe with him. He was even thoughtful in ways such as bringing food over for a meal and clearing dirty dishes from the table. He had my family over to his house for steak barbecue. All of that really attracted me to him, and after about a month we started to talk about getting married after I graduated. But being only seventeen, it was happening so *fast for me, and I began to get nervous and doubt. I'd not felt like that before, especially in such a short time, and I started to have second thoughts. It was all so much to take in that I began to wonder, Do I really love him? and I began to feel unsure of the relationship, probably because I felt unsure of myself with these emotions being so new to me. My hesitance got to the point that when he called, I'd tell Mom I didn't want to talk to him. Then he sent me a bouquet of flowers—which no one had ever done before that I recall—but I still didn't respond. Then shortly after, he stopped by the house. My mom let him in, and he came upstairs to my room and really turned on the charm. He told me everything that was good about us and how much he loved me. One thing's for sure, Tim was and is a good salesman, and he gave it all he had—he literally sold me on "us." (Now when he tries to be the salesman I know he is, I catch on pretty quick and say, "I know what you're doing, Babe. Stop it!" He doesn't have to sell me on us anymore. I'm all in.)*

We went back into a whirlwind of drinking—staying sober didn't last long—having sex, and seeing each other as much as possible for the next month or so. Then one late November afternoon not long after I turned eighteen, a friend who was dating Brian and I stopped by Tim's house before he got home. We drank some beer and talked, and by the time Tim arrived, I was buzzed. As soon as he got in the door, I met him and took him to his bedroom. We didn't have much time as I needed to get home. I can't even remember how I got home, but I do remember that as I entered the house, I thought my parents were in bed, so I walked into the kitchen for a glass of water. But my mom came downstairs and walked into the kitchen too. As I got my drink, she asked where I had been. I said, "Shannon and I went to the library and got some ice cream," and as I turned around, I stared straight down because I didn't want her to look into my eyes—I knew she'd see right through me.

At that moment, she reached for my blouse, tugged at the front of it, and said, "What is this?" I looked down to see my shirt was inside out!" Then she yelled for my dad. "George! Get down here and see your daughter!"

Dad came bouncing down the stairs and looked me over. Then he reached for the phone and said, "I'm calling Tim!" Tim answered the phone, and he didn't lie—he told Dad I had already been drinking when he got home, so that got him off the hook. But Mom was still upset and said, "George, go get Kathy a suitcase," so he did and handed it to me. Then Mom told me to go to my room and take whatever I needed because they were not going to deal with this anymore. I had to move out.

As I walked up to my room all I could think to do was throw random items into the case. I hadn't seen this coming—my parents had been concerned about my behavior, but what Mom was doing felt out of the blue—so I was a bit in shock and couldn't think clearly about what to take. I just remember grabbing stuff—mostly things Tim had given me. I also made a quick call to Tim to come get me, saying, "My parents are kicking me out of the house. I have nowhere to go, I don't know what to do. What am I going to do?!"

After we hung up, Dad came to take the suitcase downstairs for me, and he didn't say anything. I remember Mom crying as he set the case outside the front door, and as I walked out, he shut it behind me. I was stunned.

I had no idea what to do except wait for Tim. I had never lived with a guy, and this didn't feel right. But I felt I had no other choice. I was raised that living with a guy before marriage was wrong, so it was hard to understand why my parents were pushing me this way.

———

After getting the call from Kathy's dad, I wasn't surprised to get a call from her, yet I wasn't expecting her parents to throw her out of the house! Of course, I let her stay with me, but I admit I was nervous about how long it would be. I wasn't in the mind space for her to move in long-term, and that's what I was afraid of, as was Brian.

As it turned out, she stayed two nights with me then one night in a hotel before being able to go back home. And it wasn't long into December that I found out the news . . .

Kathy's mom called and said I should come over. I knew she'd taken Kathy to the doctor's office for a pregnancy test, and the results were in. When I arrived, I went downstairs where Kathy turned to me and said, "Tim, I'm pregnant . . . and you don't have to marry me . . ." As I took in the news, I said, "Of course I will marry you." Kathy's mom and dad knew we wanted to get married, but the talk was for it to happen after she graduated. But with this news, her mom said, "Looks like we'll be moving the wedding date up!" So we moved it to February 5, 1982. Five months and five days after we met, we got married and Kathy dropped out of high school.

In Case You Were Wondering . . .
TIM

What I was thinking when Kathy said she was pregnant . . . the abortion I had paid for a few years before came into my mind. I immediately thought that *this* kid needed my last name.

One of the things I want to point out about my parents during this time was how supportive they were of me. They told me I had options. If I wasn't ready to get married, I could have and keep the baby and live with them, or I could have the baby and give it up for adoption. But one thing that was not *an option was an abortion. I'm thankful—and I know Tim is too—that they took that stance and protected the sanctity of the life that I carried.*

For me, given the fact that I had paid for an abortion several years before, it wasn't an option for me either. I wanted this baby to have life and to have a name—the Bush name. In my heart and mind, things would be different with this pregnancy. As far as the rest of my lifestyle being different? Plenty happened before the wedding day that set the course of projection for our marriage—starting with continuing my bad habits with women and my need to control everything.

In Case You Were Wondering ...
KATHY

What I thought when I found out I was pregnant at eighteen . . . after my initial shock, my first thought was, "Now I can drop out of school. My mom did it, so my parents should have no problem with me doing it." To this day, dropping out of high school is one of my biggest regrets. If I could do it all over again, I would have stayed in school, even as a pregnant married girl. Dropping out of school put me into a pattern of quitting. Much later in life, Tim taught me about integrity and sticking things out.

There wasn't much time to plan the wedding given the new date, but that didn't stop me from making time to keep playing the field. In fact, I had been seeing my ex-girlfriend plus at least one other woman right up to the time Kathy and I got married. I was on a mission to sow all my oats before the wedding, then I'd stop because I literally thought that after I got married, if I had crazy good sex eight or nine times a week and someone to take care of all my needs—like wash my clothes and cook my meals—it'd keep me from straying. I wouldn't want or need other women. That tells you where my mind was!

In the meantime, I planned a three-day honeymoon trip at the beach, and I looked forward to Kathy being everything I expected as my wife.

After the wedding, Tim and I drove to Astoria, Oregon, to have pizza en route to Seaside Beach. I never liked going to the beach in February, but it's where Tim wanted to go, so that's what we did. And even though the weather was gloomy, rainy, and cold, I was excited to be married. I wouldn't have to go back home to my parents. I was all grown up, at least I thought, so I was overcome with new feelings of freedom. Unfortunately, those feelings didn't last long.

Now that I was pregnant the fun of us drinking together was gone—Tim was on his own in that department. After we ate pizza for dinner, Tim drove us to the condo and brought in groceries he'd packed in a cooler. I don't remember much about the condo except that it felt as dark and cold on the inside as it was on the outside. What I do remember, though, was the kitchen. Tim rented a place with a kitchen and expected me to cook! I didn't know much about cooking, especially for my husband. Even if I had, his expectation for a honeymoon celebration did not match mine. So here I am, two months pregnant, and not feeling well physically at all. I knew I needed to let Tim have sex—how could I keep that from him on our wedding night? This was the first time in our relationship I felt empty after sex. I knew things were not going to be what I thought as a married woman and I wondered, Did I make a mistake?

The next day we drove to Lincoln City and spent the next two nights at a hotel called Sea Gypsy. And as our trip came to an end and we had to drive home, a depressed feeling came over me—it was not the honeymoon I had envisioned. Sadly, this was only the beginning of what married life with Tim would be like.

There I was, a new wife and a soon-to-be mother, and I didn't have a clue about how to be either. And I soon found out that Tim didn't know how to be a husband either.

WHAT ABOUT YOU

More times than not, no matter how well they plan, newly married couples are so in love, they discover shortly after saying "I do" there is a lot about being a husband or wife they don't know how to navigate. Expectations, miscommunications, or how about *no* communication about the deeper things—all of it can leave them wondering, *Did I make a mistake?! This is not what I signed up for! Did I marry the wrong person?*

Can you relate?

Well, you are not alone. After all the honeymoon bliss is over (sometimes sooner rather than later), marriage can change from being an anticipated joy into what feels like plain hard work—and making a daily choice to remain committed.

In our case, we were so focused on reacting to my pregnancy and making me an "honest woman," we were naïve about the reality of what marriage really meant. I thought being married to Tim would look like my mom and dad's marriage, but I was wrong—I simply didn't know any better. Tim didn't have a good mom-and-dad example to emulate. He had his grandparents, and their roles weren't exactly the best example for what a healthy, vital, fulfilling marriage looked like.

Can you relate?

Please let me reiterate, you are not alone. What a good marriage looks like can be different for every couple, and that's okay. What matters most is your commitment to figuring out together what works for you.

Earlier I said I needed to let Tim have sex with me on our wedding night. But where did I learn that? Sex is a mutual act, so I should have never felt obligated to have it, even then. It took me many years to learn that sex is a gift in marriage, not an obligation. Are you and your spouse enjoying sex as a gift? Have you talked about this?

QUESTIONS FOR TRANSFORMATION————

- Probably more people have poor examples of what a good marriage looks like than we realize. But the truth is, the model of marriage we observe has a direct reflection on how we act in our own marriage. What do your examples look like? How are they different from your spouse's? Consider sharing one or two if you haven't already, and strive to gain understanding of each of your differences. Make sure you are giving your spouse room to speak. (More on this in chapters 16–18.)

- It's not uncommon to have some misconceptions about marriage; this is why you have pre-marriage classes. The pastor that married us said we needed to take them in order for him to marry us, but we only went to one of six. We needed *all six and more*. What are some misunderstandings or disappointments you have faced? What are some your spouse has had about you? Will you consider an honest discussion with each other to learn more about your differences in this area in a way you both feel heard? This took us over thirty years to do. Don't wait!

6

Our First Years: Not What We Expected

When Tim and I got married, I thought I'd found the man who'd love me and take care of me as I had wanted and planned through high school. I'd "arrived" and thought I would be happy—after all, it's what my mother had done, and she seemed happy. Unfortunately, this wasn't the case for me. Not only was the honeymoon Tim planned not quite what I had hoped, but the reality of being married brought challenges I never saw coming.

There I was, Mrs. Tim Bush, yet from day one, I didn't feel like a wife in the way I had expected. I thought most women looked forward to "nesting" and creating a warm, homey environment for themselves and their husbands, but I struggled with not wanting to do anything. Some of the reason was probably my hormones from being pregnant, but I felt down, even depressed, and that seemed to be the theme of my life—being married didn't change that. I had always looked for some thing or someone to make me happy, and since I was now married with a baby on the way, I thought I'd feel different, but I didn't. I definitely was not going to tell anyone how I felt either, so I slowly started to isolate myself.

Tim had his own adjustments to deal with. He worked a lot of hours in the car business. I would wake up, and he'd be gone. I would go to bed at night, and he still wasn't home. Tim made a decent income, but it bothered him that my family didn't think it was a worthy or reputable career path. We talked about a career change, which meant moving two thousand miles away . . .

Kathy's right: I did care about what her family thought of me, and having a respectable career was important to them—the car business wasn't a family fit. When I heard that Kathy's sister and brother-in-law went to Roswell, New Mexico, to attend Eastern New Mexico University to train for the oil field business, I was intrigued. There was a 99 percent chance for job placement right out of the gate, so the risk factor was low, plus a career change would make me a better guy to Kathy's parents, so we decided to prepare for the move.

In the meantime, we sold my house and moved in with Kathy's parents until our new daughter, Tricia, arrived. She finally came late on September 3 after a very traumatic birth.

To put it bluntly, Tricia was an 8-pound, 12-ounce baby that came out breech, and I had no medication! It was, indeed, traumatic, and I literally thought it was God's way of punishing me for having sex outside of marriage! Needless to say, I was grateful for my mom's help, plus I had a comfortable place to heal. I also liked caring for a baby. I had always liked babies and I felt good about having one of my own, so I liked my new role as a mom. We were very thankful for the time we had with Mom and Dad—I learned a lot from Mom about how to care for Tricia. But after three weeks of recovery, we had lived at their house for three months total, and Tim and I knew it was time to move out and head to Roswell.

Yes, we had lived with Kathy's parents for three months. That said, I was anxious to get going and start the college classes I'd signed up for. We had a two-thousand-mile drive ahead of us, so it would still be a while before we even got to Roswell. The best part was, we would have family waiting there too.

I admit, it's kinda fun to think back on that trip and just how poor we were, yet how we got by. To start, I spent $1,800 on a 1969 GMC twenty-six-foot, cab-over box truck that needed some minor repairs, which I did myself. After I refurbished it, Kathy's mom helped to clean it, then I painted it, and finished it off with a little $99 boombox. For Tricia's seat, I took a wooden apple box, bolted it down on the shelf behind our seats, and stuck a pillow inside for her to lie on. And that's how we drove across the country.

The cool part was that after we got to Roswell, I sold the truck for $2,500 and used some of the money to buy Kathy a '74 Dodge Dart for $1,000. We had already brought a Suzuki 400 motorcycle for me to use for work. If we didn't make such a profit, I'm not sure what we would have done because we were *broke*.

At first, we lived with Kathy's sister and brother-in-law. Right away I started school and got a part-time swing shift job at Wholesome Bakery to help pay bills, plus I worked overtime whenever I could. After a short time, we moved into our very first cinder block base housing duplex, which cost $300 a month, so even with overtime, we still didn't have much left to live on. I soon got a better-paying job at a place called TMC, building Greyhound buses, but that only lasted eighty-nine days. That probably sounds funny, but it's because they'd have to provide benefits at ninety days, so they'd let everyone go when they reached the eighty-nine-day mark.

This was the time when we had to heat our duplex by turning the dryer vent hose toward the inside and putting a nylon stocking over it so the hot air could warm us. Plus, we were very thankful to have a warm waterbed. We had so little money, we could hardly afford to pay attention. In fact, at Christmastime, Pop sent us a box filled with winter coats, and in the bottom of the box was a check for $250. To celebrate, we went to a Mexican restaurant and spent $20 on burritos with all the fixings and two margaritas. It was the first time we had gone out for a meal in months.

When the Greyhound job ended, Kathy said that her sister and brother-in-law had so much more food in their house because they signed up for food stamps, so of course, it made sense for us to do the same. Kathy put on one of my jackets and wrapped it shut around Tricia in front of her while sitting behind me on the motorcycle, and I drove us all to the welfare office. We sat down at a desk where a lady pushed what seemed like a one-inch stack of paperwork in front of me to fill out. I looked at the pile of paper, looked at Kathy, then back at the lady and said, "No thanks, I'll just get another job!" and we walked out. That's exactly what I did; I went on to get a job selling motorcycles while still carrying twenty-two credit hours at school.

In spite of not having money, we both look back on that time and smile. We were so close, and our marriage was good. We worked together to figure out how to make do with what we had—even to the point of Tim bleaching my hair with a cap and a crochet needle. I only wish our time there had lasted longer. After about seven months, the oil industry quickly became depressed to the point where instead of having 99 percent chance at job placement after school, there was a 1 percent chance. We both had also become homesick for our family, so by the following spring, we returned to Vancouver, WA, and Tim went into real estate . . . and immediately went back to working long hours, going back to bars, and womanizing—his secret life.

In Case You Were Wondering . . .
KATHY

About our decision to move to Roswell . . . one of the best things we did for our marriage was to move there. It was our time to leave and to cleave to each other. Our problem was that we came home too early and slid right back into our old patterns. We both wanted change, but we didn't want it badly enough to be uncomfortable.

With the continued pattern of Tim working and being gone until all hours, I struggled with feeling unloved and bored without him there. We quickly lost the emotional connection and intimacy we'd had in Roswell. Sex also seemed empty and more just all about Tim. I didn't know how to talk to him about it, or really about any part of our marriage. I had no one else to talk to either, so I kept all my thoughts inside and felt isolated. That's when I decided to call an old boyfriend just to talk and catch up—that's all I wanted to do. Only a few minutes after he answered my call and I was starting a conversation, Tim walked in, and I hung up. He asked who I was talking to, and when I said my old boyfriend's name,

Tim knew who he was and was devastated and angry (yes, even though he'd been unfaithful so many times, which I didn't find out about until years later).

I told him I was sorry, but the next day when I got home from work after picking up Tricia from Mom and Dad's, I walked into our apartment and thought it felt weird, only at first, I couldn't figure out why. Then I noticed that some furniture was missing. Where we had two chairs, there was only one. And the couch was missing. I walked into the kitchen and opened cabinets and drawers and saw that half of all the dishes, half the silverware, even one of our two knives was missing! The only "pair" of anything that was still intact was the washer and dryer. I was so distraught, not only for Tim being upset over a phone call the day before, but because now he was gone. We didn't even talk about anything, there was no discussion—he just left. I couldn't believe he was leaving me over a phone call! I didn't know what else to do but take Tricia and move back home with my parents. We stayed separated for two weeks before I found out more news that added a twist: I was pregnant again.

After telling Tim the news, we decided to get back together and keep working on our marriage. By then, Tim was already doing well enough for us to buy our first home, and it turned out to be one of the nicest houses on the block. But even with that, I continued to struggle with feeling alone since Tim worked and controlled me so much. At least I had another baby to look forward to, and in June, TJ (Tim Jr.) was born. I'm glad to say his birth was a piece of cake compared to Tricia's, and life went on as usual.

We had been going to the Lutheran church off and on all along. We even baptized Tricia and TJ because it's what I was taught to do growing up in the church. We were searching and *doing what we thought we were supposed to do to be a family, yet our lives and the cycles we fell into didn't change. They only continued to worsen.*

After trying real estate for a while, I decided to go back into what I knew best: the car business, which meant longer hours. I worked six days a week and was on call on the seventh. If it was five o'clock and I was in the middle of a deal, I didn't leave, I stayed until everything got wrapped up. Then I'd go drinking and occasionally meet women while Kathy stayed home with the kids.

Soon into the following year, I became pregnant again with our third child, and as the pregnancy progressed, Tim's party habits got pretty bad. It was November 2—a Saturday night— when he left straight from work to go to a Halloween party at a friend's house. I was at home alone with the two kids and feeling like I could have the baby any minute. Fortunately, my brother and sister-in-law came over to be with me, and I'm so glad they did. I went to put a movie into the VCR and felt a pain and wondered if I might be in labor. When I sat down and the movie started playing, I had another pain and knew then that the baby was coming.

I gave my brother the number for Scotty's house, knowing Tim was at his party.

Yeah, I remember working late, then going to Scott's house for a party in his basement. I planned to be there for maybe a few hours and got right into snorting cocaine, smoking pot, and of course, drinking, when suddenly his mom came downstairs and said, "Tim, you need to call home right now!" So I called Kathy, and she said she was in labor.

Tim got home about eleven o'clock, and when he walked in and looked at me, I could tell right away that he was high and drunk. There I was, having our third baby, and he was not in any shape to really be there for me. Plus I was so embarrassed that my brother and sister-in-law saw Tim like that.

Tim drove me to the hospital—while intoxicated—and arrived by 11:45 when they wheeled me into the delivery room. And at 1:15 a.m., November 3, 1985, Blake was born.

Of course, I was excited about Blake being born, but shortly after I got the hospital bill, the responsibilities I carried really hit me. At that moment, I felt like I had a ball and chain tied to my ankles. There I was at twenty-four, we had a nice house, cars in the driveway, and now another child to support. I really felt a heavy weight, not to mention I had financial goals I wanted to reach by the time I turned thirty, and I could see they just weren't going to happen. I always thought that in order to reach them, I wouldn't get married until I was at least thirty, but in reality, all my goals were gone. I had sacrificed my aspirations for having and providing for a family.

Everything I had dreamed of and wanted was over. I'd married Kathy before the time I swore I'd get married, and now we had three kids to take care of. I knew I couldn't quit—that would mean failure—but I felt panicked. I think now I may have had a mild anxiety attack but didn't know that's what it was. I just knew I had to try and figure out how to be a dad and a husband within the amount of hours I had left after working all day. In addition to that, my mindset was that once I left the office, I was finished. I thought *my* job was the important job, and when I got home, everything else was Kathy's job.

Needless to say, Tim didn't even help with diaper changes. The most he did was carry the dirty diapers to the washing machine. By the time Tricia was two, TJ was eighteen months, and then I had Blake as a baby, I remember running around the house trying to keep up after the kids and everything else while holding and nursing Blake. When I took him in for his well-baby checkup, the doctor saw that he wasn't gaining weight; he looked at me and said, "You've got your hands full, don't you? You're not taking the time you need to nurse like you should." I felt terrible, yet I told him I just couldn't sit long enough with all that I had to do. So he convinced me to switch to a bottle. That seemed like an easy solution, yet it carried some feelings of failure, like I wasn't being a very good mother, when I was just trying to do the best I could.

So at twenty-two, I went into the next year working hard simply to adjust to having three kids and finding some kind of balance, because I didn't get much of a break with Tim gone all the time. For him, it was life as usual—and a lot of it didn't include me.

Thoughts from the Kids . . .
TJ

I don't ever remember anything being bad at home. I felt like mom always gave us structure and routine. We would have breakfast, lunch, and dinner together, stuff like, Spa-ghettiOs with green beans, a piece of buttered toast, a yogurt, and a glass of milk. It always felt as if she was try-ing to hit as many food groups as possible. We would go to church. Go on vacation. Growing up felt like whatever a "normal" family was. If she was struggling, I never saw it.

WHAT ABOUT YOU?

Most of us believe that the more we have, the happier we'll be. Yet in New Mexico—while young and broke—we had one of our happiest times together. We couldn't afford to go out, so we spent time with each other. When we did get a little extra, we celebrated together with gratitude. Even though we didn't have a lot, our needs were met, and we both look back and think about how rich life was back then. It was a time we leaned into each other and got creative with what we had, but that happiness ended when we moved back to our old habits and lifestyle. Being successful financially isn't a bad thing, but the time and energy it takes to do so can become a wedge in marriage if we're not careful.

Kathy's right. It's also easy for a person to think that after he or she has provided for their family each day, their job ends, and that is so far from the truth! Being present and available for physical and emotional support is vital for any meaningful relationship, especially marriage. Finding a good balance is so key.

Then there is the loss of a dream—it was hard for me to face the fact that I wasn't going to reach certain goals by a certain age. My dreams were conceived prior to marriage and didn't change much over time—they were actually pretty selfish dreams at that point. Dreams and goals are good to have, but life happens, and they can get lost in the process of holding yourself and your family together. The good news is new dreams can arise out of your new circumstances, not to mention you can create them with your spouse rather than on your own, the way I had.

QUESTIONS FOR TRANSFORMATION————————

- Do you have thoughts that if only you had more, you'd be happier? If so, talk together about what it is you really want, and why. So often we go after things or more money to fill a void that can never be filled materially, yet we settle for trying.

- Do either of you have a dream that's slipping away or lost altogether? Consider sharing what you long for, draw from each other's encouragement for the acceptance life has brought, and perhaps dream together about something new.

- How do your goals line up with your family situation now versus prior to marriage? Do you both have goals or just one of you? Why or why not?

- What are you doing to invest in your marriage that builds up your relationship? Do you need help in this area? Who could you agree to ask? Come up with one or two people and set up a chat as couples, but never one-on-one with the opposite sex.

7

More Than a
Wake-Up Call

Thinking back, recalling the hills and valleys of my life journey, I can certainly see God's love and patience with my wandering and bad decisions. But there are some points where it's clear His hand was on me in ways I didn't see at the time. He used those moments to lovingly steer me toward Him without an iron fist, but rather by getting my attention in exactly the ways that spoke loudest to my heart. This point in my life was one of those times. A guy just can't keep working so hard at his career, bearing the responsibility of being a husband and raising three kids, carousing, taking drugs, and drinking in excess without something adverse happening.

Fortunately, this story has a good ending. No, I didn't turn to God through it, but I did begin to think more seriously about the consequences of my choices—not only for me, but for Kathy and my family.

It was November of 1986, and at twenty-five, I was making lots of money as a finance manager at Vancouver Nissan, doing well enough to go to nice parties and even get away for weekends. I could pretty much do whatever I wanted that money could buy. By that time, I also weighed over 290 pounds, which was the heaviest I had ever been.

Since Kathy's twenty-third birthday was approaching, I planned a weekend getaway in Lincoln City, Oregon, to celebrate. I intended to drive us in my brand-new black Maxima SE, stocked with a case of Asti Spumante and an eight ball of cocaine (that's three-and-a-half grams). We'd arranged to take the kids to Kathy's parents' house so her mom could take care of them, then leave from there for a nice hotel room on the coast.

As we ventured out of town toward Lincoln City, we stopped along the way and started drinking the wine and snorting the cocaine. In fact, we'd emptied ten of the twelve bottles by the time we got to the coast for dinner (of course, I drank most of them!). That night we went to Moe's and had their famous clam chowder and more drinks to top it off, then as we drove back to the hotel, I started not to feel so good and told Kathy, "Whoa, I'm having chest pains."

At first I thought it could have been anxiety like I'd experienced mildly a few times before, but no, it felt different. Then my heart started beating so fast and hard, I looked down and I could see it pumping right out of my chest. It's as though it was locked in at high speed and I couldn't get it to slow down. I knew I was in bad shape, and it scared me that I'd gotten so high I couldn't control what was suddenly happening to me.

In Case You Were Wondering ...
TIM

What was going on in my head at twenty-five years old . . . I thought I was going to die. from losing control because of my bad choices, to trying to fix things in real time. Living just wasn't an option. My life seemed over, and there was not going to be a tomorrow.

By the time we arrived at our room, it was about eleven o'clock and the low-forties temperature felt pretty cool outside, so I went out on the deck to see if the cold air would help clear my head and make a difference. It didn't. Then by about midnight, I got the bright idea to take a bong hit of Kona buds (weed) thinking it would help me to calm down. That tells you how messed up my thinking was! And instead of coming down, I got even *worse*.

I decided to take a cool shower to see if that would help, and I just kept thinking, *I've got to come down, I've got to come down* . . . but the shower didn't help either. By that point it hit me even harder that this was *not good*—I just might die. Finally, by two o'clock in the morning, I said to Kathy, "I gotta go to the hospital!"

It had been quite the evening, that's for sure. I was excited for a weekend away from the kids. They were still pretty young, and I didn't get many breaks. I thought it was going to be a great birthday, especially with all the wine and cocaine—something we did once in a while. We thought the combination would make for a good party.

It started out great all right, but between the drive back to the hotel and Tim's anxiety over his heart rate, the night changed quickly from celebratory to panicky—so much so that Tim's mind went into what he wanted me to say and do after he died.

While he took a shower, he spoke to me through the curtain and told me what to tell the kids and my parents so they wouldn't think anything bad of him. He kept saying, "This is what you need to do. This is what you need to do." Remember, I was high too, just not anywhere to the degree he was. I was getting scared and wondered what I was going to do if something happened to Tim. He was supposed to take care of me, so I couldn't believe he was talking about what to do after he died. I tried hard to listen to what he told me, but he was really starting to frighten me.

But then he said something that sobered me up pretty quick. "You're gonna have to take me to the hospital!" But I didn't know where a hospital was—he was always the one to do things and take care of situations like this, not me. I said, "I don't know how to get to the hospital! I can't do this!" The thought of it was terrifying.

It's only natural I thought Kathy should drive since I was in such bad shape, but when she got behind the wheel and I glanced over at her . . . it looked as though her eyes were spinning. So we changed places and at 2:30 in the morning, I drove us around Lincoln City trying to find a hospital sign. (Remember, this was long before GPS or smartphones.) I even looked for a cop, thinking he or she could get me there faster.

I finally found a blue "H" sign to follow and when we got there, I pulled up to the entrance, walked in, went to the people behind the counter, and said, "Hey, I tried something somebody on the street sold me, it was a half a gram of cocaine, and I've never tried it before, and I think I'm OD-ing on it!" They quickly took me back to a room to lay me down.

When we got to the hospital, I went in and sat down in the waiting area while Tim talked to the nurses and I thought, Here I am, twenty-three years old, and I don't even know how to talk to these people or how to handle this kind of situation. Tim always did everything. Then I thought, What am I going to do if he dies?! I didn't even know where I was.

In Case You Were Wondering . . .
KATHY

What I thought while sitting in the waiting room . . . Here I am at twenty-three, a mom to three small children, and I was totally dependent on my husband for everything. I couldn't seem to do or think for myself. I knew at this moment It was not a healthy place to be. Even during Tim's overdose, I felt like a child and so ashamed. In my shame I had no one to call for help. I just sat there hoping for the best and that I would never have to tell of this dark secret—a secret Tim and I would bury for many years. Little did I know that in order to truly break free, all our secrets would have to surface and be revealed eventually.

In the room, they covered me with a warm blanket, hooked me up to an EKG, and took my heart rate; it was 161 beats per minute lying down—and that had been the case for the past three hours. Then I told the nurse, "I gotta pee!" "Well," she said, "I can't let you get up or go out of the room, so you're going to have to wait." But I said, "I'm gonna pee in my pants!" So she gave me one of those urinal bottles to use and I proceeded to fill it up all the way. They handed me another one and filled it up too. Then I started on a third one when I was finally done. It was probably all that Asti Spumante!

After some time passed, a truly significant moment came while I lay on my bed and tried to settle down. A lady on one side of me was dying from emphysema, and a twelve-year-old on the other side of me needed emergency appendectomy surgery. And there was only one doctor on call.

There I was, a drug user, lying in between two life-and-death situations that were not by choice, yet mine was. I felt convicted about how senseless my situation was compared to theirs. I could see how I had taken for granted the value of everyday life and failed to protect it. I was also overcome with guilt—I had let Kathy and my family down and left all the consequences on her shoulders to clean it up if I didn't make it. That's not something I wanted to do.

Finally, at 8:30 that morning, I was released to leave, and when I got up and went into the lobby, the sunlight shined through the windows as I walked up to Kathy. I could tell she was still wired from the cocaine and saw that her face was filled with worry. I thought to myself, *What have I done?*

I took her hand, and we walked out to the car together. We didn't say anything. We were so sobered up by the experience, we could hardly speak.

I never touched cocaine again.

WHAT ABOUT YOU?

Have you ever found yourself slipping into a habit that escalated to the point of being out of control? When Tim and I first started using cocaine, it was once every two or three months—we thought, what's the harm in that? I even thought it was bringing us closer because I had so much to say to Tim when we used it. All I had bottled up inside came out with cocaine. But then we started doing it once a month. Then occasionally every other week. It's a good example of how we justified doing something that was harmful— even illegal—because it was only once in a while. It slowly worked its way into our lives and almost cost Tim his life.

Yeah, not to mention how expensive it was. Last chapter I touched on my broken dream of financial success by the age of thirty, yet I spent so much on our habits, I could have used the same money to make some wise investments and at least attain part of my dream. Instead, I wasted our extra money on drugs and alcohol. I also didn't consider how the consequences of my actions would affect Kathy and my family, or even the doctor who was on call to treat more life-threatening conditions. I needed to make some lifestyle changes, and "no more drugs" was the change in my mind— but not much else.

QUESTIONS FOR TRANSFORMATION———

- Our drugs of choice happened to be cocaine, alcohol, and weed. Harmful habits can come in all shapes and sizes, colors, and forms: overeating, compulsive shopping, looking at inappropriate things on the internet, and many more. Can you identify any vices you have that could hold the power to encroach on your life in a negative or harmful way? If so, do you believe you'll be able to kick them on your own? Or will you be brave to discuss what they are and consider a healthier alternative? Once you share, you are on track to capture them, and whatever they are, you'll have a good chance of ending them.

- Are you doing anything unhealthy that is keeping your marriage relationship from growing? Can you share it right now with your spouse?

- It is so important to be disciplined with our resources, especially when we're trying to reach a goal or fulfill a dream, and when every decision we make has a ripple effect on those around us. Are you careful to consider the ripple effect your decisions make on your loved ones? Even on your very life?

8

I Want Out!

After experiencing such a close call with death, I really started to rethink life and mortality—not something a successful guy in his twenties normally thinks about. But it sealed the deal for me to do something to slow down and live a simpler life. I started the process of looking for a different job, determined to find one that would pay more while working less. Soon, I ended up getting hired by a company called Adesco, and was moved to Puyallup, Washington, just south of Seattle. The job meant less hours, the potential for more money, and, in turn, a slower pace.

At first, Kathy and I thought it was worth the effort to move because, even though the job meant I had to travel, I was still able to slow down from the daily pressures, plus I excelled in my work. But the money wasn't growing as promised, which didn't help with reducing the anxiety I struggled with. I just couldn't put it to rest. At the same time, hindsight shows that the circumstances were yet another point when God popped in and made Himself known to me through my new boss, Mike. I realized early on that he was a Christian—although a different kind of Christian than me—because he often talked about God, and at times he would even say to me, "Tim, the Lord has something planned for you, something beyond what you're doing here." I didn't know how to take what he meant, so I'd say, "Whatever, Mike!" and shrug it off. I just knew I was glad he was with me on the day I got another wake-up call about my lifestyle choices.

In Case You Were Wondering . . .
TIM

My state of mind while talking with Mike while drinking multiple cups of coffee . . . I was feeling stressed about not making enough money, being incredibly overweight, carrying the burden of having to stay in control, and not sharing my past indiscretions—all of it was overtaking me and deep down left me feeling useless. I literally had no self-worth for the first time as an adult—or even as a boy. My life was very childish. It put my anxiety even higher when it looked like giving up a few things must happen. Of course, I thought making more money was the biggest issue and the answer to fixing it all.

Mike and I had been working in Fife, Washington, and one morning we stopped at a coffee shop. As we sat and talked over several cups of coffee, I suddenly felt *anxious*. As I've mentioned, I'd experienced other milder moments of anxiety before, but this time it was much more pronounced. Then, not long after the symptoms began, my entire left arm went numb, and without hesitating, I looked at Mike and said, "I don't feel right! I think I'm having a heart attack!"

There I was, only twenty-six years old, thinking I was having a heart attack. I was scared that, once again, I couldn't control my body and what was happening to me, even though this time I hadn't taken drugs, which made it even more confusing. I did not like it or the lack of control.

Mike immediately took me to the closest hospital, and when they wheeled me in, they did the standard tests and found I was having a full-blown anxiety attack, which can feel just like a heart attack. I was relieved, yet I just wanted to get it under control and get out of there, so they gave me a quaalude to calm me down and released me shortly afterward.

Our time in Puyallup was a season of unrest for me as well. Not only was Tim having anxiety, but I was also struggling, only in a different way. His new job required him to travel more than before, which meant I was on my own to an even greater degree to manage and take care of the kids and the house. This wasn't new to me, but being alone at night was, and it's when I began to develop a fear unlike I'd ever felt. I couldn't sleep or relax out of fear that someone would break in and attack me. It was so unsettling.

We had started attending the local Lutheran church—the pastor even counseled us a little—so I decided to see if he might have some advice about how I might cope or even overcome my growing fear of being alone. But my experience with him was even more confusing than helpful. When I shared the situation, he listened and then told me that when fear started to come over me, to act like a mama bear. He said to get a bat and hold it while I went through the house. I literally, thought, What?! There was no spiritual counsel, which I had expected from a pastor. I felt pretty much on my own to deal with my fear. I thought a church was supposed to help in times like this, so I was disappointed by the experience.

In the meantime, Tim showed more signs of anxiety, which didn't help matters, and it was shortly after his false heart attack when we learned that his grandmother's husband, Howard, had passed away. With all the help that she needed, Tim felt even more pressure and anxiety and need for money. He even thought that the lack of money might have been the cause of all the anxiety—not the lifestyle he'd been living—so he decided to take yet another job in Tri-Cities, all the way across Washington, to manage and grow a car dealership. This meant relocating and getting the pay we needed and the hope that both of us would settle down more into a calmer frame of mind. But the move there was the beginning telltale sign of even worse things to come regarding Tim's health. His anxiety was so bad, he couldn't even help with our move—the most he could do was lie on a couch and watch. He was practically useless. My thoughts were—and I kept them to myself—Can't he see that he needs to lose weight?

It was humiliating not to be able to help move my family, to lie down on a couch and watch Kathy and her family and my family, who came to help, do all the work. I began to realize I'd need to make some changes for a more long-term difference for my health, which I wanted. Right away we started attending the Lutheran church there, and we even taught Sunday school. I also decided to go on a weight loss diet, I stopped drinking alcohol, and I started playing racquetball. Soon the weight came off to the lowest I'd been since high school. This really helped me because by then, I could feel a difference in my well-being. The anxiety came and went only occasionally, and when it did, all I had to do was exercise or have a drink to calm down.

Unfortunately, my new and healthy look got noticed by the wrong people of the opposite sex. Add to that a renewed burst of energy, and I was on fire—for success in my new job at a big car dealership, and for returning to my ladies' man type of behavior. By this time, though, I wasn't the only one who turned to the opposite sex for fulfillment.

By the time we settled down in Tri-Cities, the kids were old enough to leave at home with babysitters, which meant Tim and I could go out more together—and we did. For the next few years, we began hanging out regularly at a karaoke bar and became friends with the people who worked there. Tim was still working long days, so when weekends rolled around, we'd go to dinner there, sometimes with friends, and run up a bar tab, and of course, sing karaoke. We became regulars at this bar. The employees all knew us by name, and we knew them. Over time, I became attracted to one of the employees, and he seemed to like me too, so I started to feel special.

When we talked, I felt like I could truly be myself. He was everything Tim wasn't, beginning with not acting like a father figure. I felt the freedom to be and feel like an adult and be accepted for me, unlike how I felt with Tim. This guy even smoked—something I could never do with Tim—so we had that in common too. I had been so lonely for so long; I began to develop feelings for him. And over time, they changed from those of a friend into an emotional force that drew me to him more and more. Soon, I began an emotional affair, which started to turn to a physical affair without going to sex. Emotional stimulation is very strong—it affects your entire being if you're not careful, and I let it flow to the fullest. It felt so good to feel seen and heard and not be manipulated or controlled.

Finally, the point came when I admitted to Tim that I loved this man. I wanted to be with him and not be married to Tim anymore. I wanted out and told Tim as much.

Of course, that didn't go over too well with him . . .

In Case You Were Wondering . . .
KATHY

This was my first affair. I see now so clearly why this happened and would change it in a minute if I could. I wanted to be loved. I wanted to be seen and heard. I just wanted to be happy, and this guy made me feel all these things. All the excitement I had felt with and for Tim were gone. I knew I had married the wrong man, so how would I ever feel good with Tim again? I even felt justified because God would want me to be happy—I was so messed up. This way of thinking continued for many more years.

WHAT ABOUT YOU?

Affairs—whether emotional or physical—can happen so quickly and easily and for a myriad of reasons. From wanting more than what we have, to falling for the lie that life would simply be better with someone else, they are a lure that destroys far too many marriages. For me, I longed to be seen and accepted for who I was—to the point of confusing infatuation (a feeling) with love (a commitment). Realistically, seeing someone only part-time in a fun environment isn't reality for having a lasting relationship. Turning to Tim and working on my marriage would have been the right thing to do.

On that note, the statistics are broad, but it would be safe to say that a large percentage of marriages are marred by infidelity. That means the possibility of many couples reading this right now could be one of the statistics. If this is you, friend, I hope you'll turn to each other and recommit to your vows. If this isn't you, please think about the situations you put yourself in and understand the sober reality that every marriage is subject to the possibility of straying apart. Being aware and taking steps to avoid these unfortunate opportunities is important.

QUESTIONS FOR TRANSFORMATION————

- Given the high statistics for marriages that have experienced infidelity, will you be honest with yourself and with your spouse about any areas you feel vulnerable to the possibility? Will you discuss and commit to any changes necessary that will decrease your chances of it happening?

- Are you doing anything that could or might be considered unhealthy? How can you change? How can your spouse support you? Put your stake in the ground and determine to work on it together.

- If you have experienced the pain that comes with an affair, will you be open to getting the help you need to work through what may have caused it and how you will both heal? Do you have the freedom as a couple to talk about this? Why or why not? Many couples can make it through the journey, with a lot of work and commitment. There is hope. And it's worth it!

9

Let Her Go

I couldn't dial the number to the karaoke bar fast enough. "*Jerry*! I just found out Kathy's been having an affair with the guy who works with you, and I'm about to come down there and let him *have* it! I'm on my way now."

When I arrived at the door, Jerry greeted me and said, "Tim, I can't just let you in here and completely rip him apart . . . but . . . I *can* let you come in and turn my back for one minute. *And* I'd need to run it by the owner before you start doing what you're going to do. How about that?"

"Okay, Jerry."

I waited and stood in disbelief. This was a guy I thought was my *friend*. I trusted him and couldn't help but think about all the evenings Kathy and I had spent there having fun with him and the other staff. *I just couldn't believe it.*

A few minutes later, Jerry came back and gave the green light, and in I stormed. I walked into the room where he was standing, grabbed him by the back of the neck and said, "You need to leave my wife *alone*. If you don't, I'm going to *rip* your head off." I said some other things as well, but I won't share them here!

When I was sure he'd gotten my message, I drove home thinking this was God's way of getting back at me. I'd been cheating on Kathy, which she still didn't know, so He was leveling the playing field—that's how God worked, right? I also thought that if Kathy did end up leaving me, this guy didn't have any money to support her, so she'd have to take the kids and move in with her parents. By the time I got home, it was late, but I couldn't settle down. I knew I was losing control, and I really needed to get it back, so I snapped at Kathy, "I'm calling your parents!" And she said, "Fine. Go ahead."

———

I picked up the phone, dialed their number, and didn't even say hello.

"You guys, I need to let you know that *your daughter is having an affair, and she wants to leave me. I don't know what you're going to do about it, but you need to figure it out!*"

Kathy's mom said calmly, "Tim, listen, I think you need to go see the pastor that married us; he's Pastor Gedde. He's at the Lutheran church in Richland. He married us over thirty years ago, so we've known him a long time, and I think that if anyone can help you, it'll be him. I think he does marriage counseling, though I'm not sure to what degree. I was so devastated and grasping at straws, I said, "Okay, I'll call him." I just knew that divorce wasn't an option for me, but I had to do something to *fix Kathy.*

The next morning, Pastor Gedde took my call right away. Years later, I'd wonder if Kathy's parents had called him to "grease the skids." After I introduced myself, he said, "Tim, I want you to come see me."

When I arrived, I sat down and was filled with a little hope and even more determination. I figured that since this guy had been a pastor for so long at the largest church in Tri-Cities, he had a direct connection with God, so I didn't waste any time. He was a big gun in my eyes and someone I needed on my side to fix Kathy.

"I'm married to Janice and George's daughter, I bought her a big house, I bought her a boat, she drives a new car, we go on vacations all the time—I mean, she has it *made*. And she's not happy." Then I told him how great I was and accentuated how messed up Kathy was. While I talked, he took some notes and didn't really say much. Then I looked at him and said, "You've got a direct connection with the Big Guy, right?! You can fix this, right?!"

He said steadily, "Well, Tim, I'll need to talk to her. Why don't you go home and ask her to come in and see me."

"Yes! I'll tell her to come see you!" And off I went to get Kathy.

When I got home, I said, "Pastor Gedde wants to see you *now*! You need to go see him." So Kathy left and I immediately felt assured that she was going to get fixed. It was going to be *better*! My trust in this man and him being connected with God was truly the answer. I was feeling pretty good at this point that he could get her straightened out and back in line.

I remember Tim walking in and saying that the pastor wanted to see me "now." He was excited that the pastor was going to fix me. So I went to the church, walked into Pastor Gedde's office, and sat down. After we said our hellos, he said, "I want to know what's going on, Kathy. Tell me about your marriage."

I shared that I'd been living with a control freak, and I didn't love him. I said, "I'm not happy and haven't been happy for a very long time. Tim thinks that because of all the stuff we have, I should be happy." Then I told him I met another guy that I love, and I don't want to be married to Tim anymore. When I said I didn't love Tim anymore, Pastor Gedde said, "We can fix that." I didn't understand what he meant, so I went on to explain all the stuff Tim had bought for me—the house, the car, the boat—and that I didn't care. Things didn't make me happy.

He said, "Okay, now I'd like for you go home and have Tim come back and see me."

And I did.

———

As I drove back to the church, I remember being *excited* that we were to this point. I trusted Kathy's mom and dad, I trusted this guy since they'd recommended him, and I just knew they were all going to be helpful. I felt good to have a wagon circle of support in my favor. So, when I arrived, I was feeling pretty cocky.

I walked back into his office, sat in the chair in front of him, and leaned back while thrusting my leg over the arm of the chair.

"Okay, Rev, what's the fix for my wife?"

He looked at me even-keeled and said, "Well, Tim, I don't know how to tell you this other than just to tell you straight that your wife doesn't love you anymore."

"Okay, well, you're connected to the Big Guy, right?! How're you going to fix her?"

"I don't think you're hearing me, Tim." He looked down and picked up a yellow Mohican pencil, wrapped his fingers around the end where the lead is, and said, "Pull this pencil out of my hand," so I pulled it out of his hand. Then he said, "That's how much control you have in your marriage right now." And I said, "Okay . . . so what's the fix?"

"I still don't think you're hearing me, Tim. You know that boat you love so much? Well, Kathy doesn't love it at all. She doesn't even like it. Think about this: you're on the boat and you have a fifty-foot life rope with a round flotation device at the end, only she's fifty-five feet out in the water drowning, and she can't get to it no matter how hard you throw it to her. That's what's going on in your marriage. She doesn't love you anymore, and you don't have any control over it."

"Okaaay . . ." I said as I brought my leg down and sat up in the chair. "I guess I understand now. What do we do? . . . What *do* we do?" He had my full attention.

"Well, this is my recommendation. You could go back and try to control everything the way you normally do, and I'm almost positive you'll lose her. Or you can go home and let her go. If she comes back to you, you'll have something to work with." He wanted me to release her to this other dude. I was now feeling a bit desperate.

"Okay, Pastor, I can do that. What else can I do?"

Then he said something no one had ever said to me before. He said, "Well, we can pray."

I was startled. I had *never* prayed other than ritual prayers at some meals. Never. Not in my whole life, even while going to church for many years, as this was never taught or modeled to me. Or maybe I just wasn't paying attention. But I said, "Okaaay . . ."

Then this six-foot-four Norwegian pastor with hands bigger than a basketball grabbed my hand, walked me over to a small altar with a padded bench where we both knelt, and prayed for me. I don't remember anything about what he said; all I could think was that this big man was holding my hand (which was odd) and praying with me. I didn't hear anything he said, but I do remember feeling something different. I was extremely uncomfortable—I was holding another man's hand and kneeling next to him at an altar and *praying* for the first time for something other than a meal. I also felt a deep sense of encouragement that something different would happen other than me controlling things.

When we finished, I got up and went home feeling scared, yet I had peace at the same time. I was not at all sure where the peace was coming from, I just knew it was there. I did what Pastor Gedde suggested; I looked at Kathy and said, "I want you to know I love you, and I'm going to be here for the kids, and you can go be with the other guy. Whatever amount of time you need, go take it. I will be here when you get back." I didn't threaten her—I wasn't even mad. I basically gave her permission to be with another man. I let her go.

When Tim said that to me, I was shocked. He was giving me freedom to be with another man. I heard love, not control, in his voice. I had always felt that if I were ever to leave, I would lose everything, including my kids. This was different and I knew he meant it. It was surreal that he gave me permission to continue the affair, which I knew was wrong. Before, he would have talked about getting a divorce and say he'd send me half the bills, but this time he said he'd keep the kids—he wasn't going to take them— and he didn't talk about taking my home from me. He said he would help me. Thinking back, it removed some of the desire in the situation! Then I remembered that growing up I had a poster in my room that said, "If you love someone set them free. If they come back, they are yours; if they don't, they never were."[1] I felt Tim had set me free for the first time in our marriage, and that was a different feeling.

As I got in my car, I felt hesitant because deep down, I really didn't want to leave. I saw something different in Tim I'd never seen before, and my feelings were changing quickly. I wasn't so sure of myself anymore. But I went ahead and left and drove around for a couple of hours trying to process what to do. And before I knew it, I was back at home. I went inside and said, "You know, I really want to be with you—I mean with the man I just saw earlier."

I called the other guy and told him Tim had said I could be with him, and he asked, "What are you going to do?" At that point, I told him I was staying with Tim—I wanted to be with the Tim that just spoke to me in a way he'd never spoken to me before.

In Case You Were Wondering . . .
TIM

What I was thinking while driving from Pastor Gedde's office to home . . . It was about a twenty-minute drive, and in my head, I went back and forth on what to say to Kathy. I don't think I was sure what I'd say until it came out of my mouth. The poster on Kath's wall about letting go of someone you love was something I never knew till writing this book. It's nice to be still learning new things after over four decades.

---

1. Richard Bach

When Kathy came back and said what she said, I couldn't help but think about how Pastor Gedde was right. I was excited that there was still a chance! But then Kathy said, "Not so fast . . . I want to work this out with you, but there's something I need to tell you. I want you to know I've been lying to you all these years about smoking. I've smoked ever since before our first date. I lied to you because you told me you didn't date girls who smoke."

What?! That was *crazy*! At that point we had been married nine years, and I never once suspected that Kathy smoked. She always smelled good; I'd never tasted them when we kissed. But even so, I said, "If you're going to smoke, I'm going to smoke with you!" And we went upstairs and smoked together. It was the first time I'd smoked a cigarette since that day with my Gram . . .

I was twelve years old, and I'd just started living with Pop and Gram. They were both chain smokers, and Gram was determined to do what she could to keep me from becoming one too. She took me in the bathroom, lit up a L&M 100 cigarette, and handed it to me. She said that if I ever wanted to smoke, she'd smoke with me, and she gave me that cigarette and made me smoke the whole thing without stopping, all the way down to the filter. By the time I finished, I literally threw up! Her plan worked because I never smoked again after that—until now. And Kathy and I smoked together for five years.

Smoking was something I'd done since I was a teenager, and it felt good to finally get it out in the open with Tim. When I say I smoked, it was two or three a day, and I didn't smoke during pregnancies or nursing. My parents smoked, but as all of us kids got older, they quit smoking in front of us. My mom would go in the bathroom and smoke by herself, so that's what I did. But when I met Tim and he said he wouldn't date a girl who smoked, I never stopped, I just did it when he wasn't home. Smoking was something I enjoyed by myself, but at the same time, I had to hide it from Tim, or else. When I could smoke with the guy I had the affair with, I felt free to be myself without hiding anything. I felt accepted even though I smoked. This guy didn't put conditions on his friendship with me.

I was surprised that Tim started doing something with me that I liked. It was clear that he was trying with me, but I couldn't help but laugh because he really didn't even know how to hold a cigarette. It was a little embarrassing when the kids finally told him he smoked like a girl! But what was bad was, now that I didn't have to hide it, we ended up smoking a lot more—for the next five years—before we stopped. Our drinking continued more too because of smoking together. My mind would travel back to the man I'd had an affair with occasionally, but I never shared that with Tim.

In Case You Were Wondering . . .
KATHY

When I finally confronted Tim about my smoking, I specifically said, "I'm going to smoke, and if you don't like it, you can leave me." Tim choosing to smoke with me was not the answer to this declaration from me—two wrongs do not make a right. I was desperately fighting for my independence, and I believe this moment was me trying to break free of Tim's control in some small way. Smoking was not the answer for either Tim or me, and once again, this was something we learned much later.

In the meantime, we started going to Pastor Gedde's church—in fact we loved going to church more than before—and we went to him for marriage counseling, which really helped. Tim kept thanking him for his "magic stuff" that he put into our marriage—no credit was given to God, yet we know now that He was very much involved. And things between us were good for the next few years.

One day, we invited Pastor to have lunch with us—ironically at the same karaoke place where all this began. We wanted to treat him, but we were taken aback that when we ordered, he ordered himself a beer. Tim and I were so surprised. We were still drinking a lot, so he must have felt it was okay to drink a beer with us. But what he didn't realize was, in our minds, that made it okay for us to drink—and alcohol remained very much a part of our story. Later, we saw him smoking and, once again, in our eyes smoking became okay, or at least, we used his actions to justify our own.

WHAT ABOUT YOU?

Thinking back, I am so grateful Kathy's mom didn't take sides and steer me down the path of leaving. Instead, she helped me fight for my marriage. Then the wisdom that Pastor Gedde provided was instrumental in helping us at a very volatile point. This speaks volumes to the importance of reaching out for help from people who are *for* your marriage more than they are going to fuel the fire and encourage you to quit. There's no telling what would have happened had we not had that.

The lesson I learned about loosening my grip of control on Kathy was huge. I received so much hope knowing she stayed because she wanted to, not because I manipulated her into staying, which is something I think we all want, right? My control was over the top. It covered up the things I was doing, since I was a quick talker and even a quicker thinker in almost any situation. My ability to go back to the things she did and garbage-dump on her helped me gain back control. It wasn't done in anger but with manipulation. I wouldn't push so far that she'd leave, but I'd pressure her by not forgiving her, which, for the most part, was something I did for another two decades.

For me, this was my first real affair, and let me stress, emotional affairs are as bad as physical ones—sometimes even harder to overcome. I had totally fallen for the lie that being with another man would make things different and better. Alcohol compromised my judgment, took away my inhibitions, and fueled my belief that I deserved to be happy, which is what the world tells us every day. And while we do deserve goodness and joy, we will never be happy when we forfeit our integrity and the commitment to work things out. Too many marriages and families are damaged and broken because of these lies.

QUESTIONS FOR TRANSFORMATION

• Every marriage takes work to some degree, and it's important to have access to sound advice when times get hard. Do you have anyone in your life who will do that? Someone who will help you off the ledge when you're ready to jump, or who won't take sides but will hold you accountable and provide encouragement for success? If not, will you make a point to find someone who will?

- It doesn't feel very good when conditions are placed on us. Boundaries are good, yes, but when we say, "I'll love you as long as you do *this* or act a certain way," we set our marriage up with unrealistic expectations. Conditions tend to choke the freedom to be ourselves, and when that happens, it's hard for true intimacy to flourish. Can you think of any conditions or ways you might manipulate your spouse to gain control over them? Or, on the other hand, do you feel like you're on the receiving end of conditional love? Will you have the courage to talk with each other candidly and try to put trust in place of control?

- Others are always watching us, especially when they respect us. Kathy and I were certainly watching Pastor Gedde because his life's work affected our marriage for the good. When he drank a beer with us, the message we heard was, "It's okay to drink." For him, having a beer wasn't wrong or a sin, but for us, drinking contributed to many of our problems. This leads to the question, What message are you sending to others? To your spouse? To your children? Will you consider taking inventory and modifying anything that could be sending a mixed or inconsistent signal?

- On a related note, are you doing anything in your life you wouldn't want your spouse to see? Your kids? Your grandkids? If you believe in God and think He sees everything, how about Him?

- Investing in your marriage is so very important, whether with a trained counselor or someone whom you respect that's been around the track a few more times than you. Do you have ideas of who might fill that need? It's important to talk together and give each other freedom to be heard.

Do one or both of you have some things to process with another couple or counselor who you think could help your marriage thrive? If so, make it a marriage goal and give it a deadline. Here are a few prompts to help you:

- Counselors or more mature couples we'd like to model after are:
    — Which one of us will set up a meeting?
    — Date we need to set it by:
    — How will we encourage each other in this process?

10

Wait! This Only Happens to *Other People*

Since meeting Pastor Gedde and working with him on our marriage and attending his church, I was glad to have some good years together with Kathy, at least for a while. I would consider it a time when life really seemed to take a turn. In addition to these changes, we even chose to start our own used car business together called Tim Bush Motor Company, which brought a lot of financial success. We were making more money, going to church regularly, and searching to be more of a normal family. And Pastor Gedde was a big influence. He even prayed at the place when we started our business, encouraged us to put an ichthus (fish) symbol on the end of the covered drive area, which we did, and he also bought several cars from us, including two Cadillacs. He even brought many of his friends and encouraged others to buy from our local family business. He became a true friend.

When I look back, though, I say with a smile that when we went to church, a big motivation was to capitalize on networking and selling more cars. I didn't know that wasn't good, I just knew it made sense to me to meet people and give them my business card and happen to mention I sell cars! In any case, it worked and my involvement in a church environment grew. I even served on the administrative board a couple times a month where I helped them get a van and plan a remodel.

I, on the other hand, didn't get so involved. I tried attending the women's ministry Bible studies, but in all honesty, I struggled with feeling intimidated, even stupid. I didn't have the knowledge they all seemed to have—even with my religious background—and no one thought to reach out and take me under their wing and help guide me. I eventually stopped trying to engage because I didn't want to appear as dumb as I felt. I just felt out of place and still struggled with being shy.

One area at church I struggled with was giving, which we started to do, but I confess it took a while. When they'd pass an offering plate during service, deep down it bothered me. I never really got the deal about giving your money away. In one of our conversations, Pastor Gedde said that when you give, you'll get it back tenfold. Kathy and I agreed to start giving $300 a month and called it our tithe. But when at the end of the year I didn't make ten times more than I made the year before, I thought Pastor Gedde had lied! I talked to him about it and said, "What's the deal? I'm pretty good at hearing, especially when it comes to the topic of money, so you were wrong!" But he explained that that wasn't how it worked and that I should keep on giving, so I did because Kathy and I trusted him.

Over time, as things went well and the money kept rolling in, I even bought Kathy her dream home, and . . . we also reverted to old patterns. We fell back into more drinking and partying and, not surprisingly, more infidelity. Kathy began an affair that lasted a few months with a man she met on a girls' weekend in Montana. He'd often come to Tri-Cities for his work, and they would hook up. We also continued the cycle of Kathy eventually confessing and me persecuting her while I kept silent about my own indiscretions. The focus was always on fixing Kathy because she wasn't a "loyal" wife. Our marriage was still pretty volatile.

Over time, Pastor Gedde retired, and this rocked our world—in fact, it broke our hearts. It was an emotional time of adjustment because we went to that church because of him, so when he left, it didn't feel the same. We know now that he was more of a draw for us than God, which is not a good motive, but we didn't understand that then, so it was difficult.

After he left, there were a series of interim pastors for three or four years before we finally got a new permanent one. The new pastor didn't last long because he had an affair with the associate pastor. It was disillusioning to learn that a pastor would have an affair, since he was supposed to be the example! Over this time, Kathy and I slipped into going to church only occasionally and would take the kids to Sunday school now and then. We knew it was important for them to go.

Then came a new long-term senior pastor. We liked him, but not long after he arrived, an unexpected bomb dropped on him, then on us, that rocked our view of the church and of God.

———————

Tim was sick with mono, so this particular Friday night we'd stayed home and were in bed when Tricia, who was then fourteen, came into our room saying she didn't feel good. Then right away she started vomiting. Naturally, I thought she was sick with the flu, so I cleaned her up and got her back into bed. The next morning, the pastor called us and said he needed to come over; there was something he needed to discuss with us. He also made sure to ask if Tricia was home.

He arrived shortly afterward and wanted to talk about Tricia's youth leader at church. He had called pastor the previous night to confess something that happened, and it involved Tricia.

The man had attended the church for a while and was a likeable, highly educated, high-level engineer who was trusted because of his solid reputation. And apparently the night before, his wife had walked in on him while he was on the phone with Tricia . . . having phone sex. The wife didn't know who was on the other line—she assumed it was another woman, not a child—so she took the phone from him and started saying hurtful things to Tricia—or the "other woman." She hadn't considered it to be a teenage girl—our little girl—from church youth group.

Once the wife got on the phone, Tricia hung up. Then the wife called again, and Tricia hung up. Then again, and again. Finally, Tricia was so distraught, she took an entire bottle of aspirin to try and kill herself—all while we were upstairs. The "flu" I thought she had was her body releasing the overdose of medication she took.

Thoughts from the Kids . . .
TRICIA

When my abuse was brought to the light, it was an extremely confusing time for me. I didn't understand what to believe. My abuser's wife assumed I was the other woman, and when she repeatedly called and accused me of being a home wrecker, I panicked. I felt lost, afraid, and hopeless. I had nowhere to turn because the relationship had been a secret. Unfortunately, I felt that ending my life was my only option. Thankfully God had bigger plans for my life, and I was ultimately unsuccessful.

Evidently, the abuse had started when Tricia was thirteen, so it had been occurring for over a year without us ever knowing. This was, and still is, hard to swallow. The one redeeming part of the story was that the husband was worried enough about Tricia and had enough of a conscience to call the pastor and tell him what had happened.

We were shocked *and heartbroken. It was especially hard since I had been abused at her age and understood the scope of consequences to come. The reality of me not protecting Tricia was the worst part. I was so concerned about me; I wasn't there for Tricia the way I normally would be.*

Pastor let us know that the youth pastor was removed from the church permanently and after a legal back-and-forth, we were not allowed to have anything to do with him—no communication, so we didn't. His initial consequence was a ninety-day work release. It was hard for us that, at first, he didn't lose his job—he didn't lose *anything*. It wasn't until later we found out he had lost plenty. It took Tricia short of twenty years to heal from the abuse, and the journey was not easy. She had literally fallen in love with the man, so when the harsh episode with his wife happened, and then he was suddenly completely out of her life, she became very rebellious.

Yeah, before all this happened, Tricia loved school, she loved church, she was a straight A student and a cheerleader. After that night, her attitude changed completely. She started drinking, doing drugs, she met with other boys, and her room was a magnified mess. And she wouldn't go to school. Because I had dropped out of school, something I made clear to Tim was that Tricia was going to finish high school—all our kids were going to finish high school! It was as though the pain set Tricia on a suicide mission—she just wanted to die. Her life was destroyed, and her actions almost destroyed our relationship. Things became so toxic. I literally had to watch over and take constant care of her for quite a while.

When Kathy expressed that she would *not* let Tricia skip school, I remember telling Tricia I was going to put her over my shoulder and go to school with her, which is exactly what I did. I got clearance from the school counselor and sat with her in all her classes for almost two days. Finally, she said, "Dad, if you leave, I will go to school"—she was *so* embarrassed. I left, and she continued to go.

Thoughts from the Kids . . .
TRICIA

Prior to my abuse, I was "the perfect child." I had straight A's, I was involved in church, I had huge dreams and goals for my life, and my parents would probably agree that I was extremely easy to parent up to that point. What started as a friendship quickly turned into an inappropriate relationship between a man and a child. I didn't have many, if any, consistent positive male relationships in my life, which probably made me an easy target. When the abuse ended and ultimately the relationship ended, my life changed dramatically. I stopped caring about anything and spiraled out of control. Outside of the initial suicide attempt, I lived my life in a way that I didn't care if I lived or died. I am thankful that my parents kept me in school and didn't make it an option to quit. Those were some of the hardest years of my life. Because of the church hurt, I was angry at God for quite some time. Looking back, I now know that God had big plans for me because he protected me and walked me through all of it even if I couldn't see Him at that time.

After we found out about the abuse, I couldn't help but think back and remember some signs that something seemed off, but I couldn't quite put my finger on it. My instincts told me Tricia was getting too "ready" and dressed for youth group before the youth leader picked her up to take her to church. He had a stepchild the same age that went to church, *so we didn't give it much thought. And when I said something to Tim, his thoughts were,* What would a forty-one-year-old man want to do with a thirteen-year-old girl?! *Of course, now we know differently, but then, it didn't make sense, so we let it go.*

In Case You Were Wondering . . .
KATHY

I remember the evening Tricia came up from her downstairs bedroom. I looked at her and thought how grown up and pretty she looked. She had some makeup on. More than usual. When the doorbell rang, and her youth leader was at the door, I knew deep down something was not quite right. It seemed he was picking her up for a date. This was a mother's intuition and I ignored it. I would come to regret this soon.

In our minds, the church was and is supposed to be a safe place, especially for children. We placed trust in the youth leader because he was in a leadership position. It was shattering for the one place we thought was safe to let us down to such a low level.

After this incident, what faith we had—in pastors, in the idea of church, in what we knew of God—went downhill. We didn't go back for a long time, and we stopped giving. After some time, we went back since the guy was no longer there, but we only went occasionally, not regularly.

In the meantime, Tim and I continued our own path of searching and going to counselors to help fix me and hold our marriage together. All the while, I didn't know that, during this time, Tim was not being transparent in counseling and was continually seeing other woman.

In Case You Were Wondering . . .
TIM

Back then, I did not know the difference between spirituality and religion, but for sure, Tricia was all that—both spiritual and religious. Never did the thought come into my mind that something like this could happen to our daughter *in church.* Everyone there seemed so perfect with dress-up clothes for women and suit and ties for men; even kids dressed up. How could this happen with what seemed like perfect people? How, as a man, could I have ever trusted what seemed to be a total lie. I'd not protected my daughter. How could a dad let this happen? My thinking at this point was that going to church had been a bad choice. The people there were a bunch of hypocrites.

WHAT ABOUT YOU?

We usually equate going to church with a secure, dependable environment, yet bad things can still happen in the one place we think should be safe. Which leads to church hurt—a lot of people won't go to church because of this. But the reality is, people in church are not perfect, even those in leadership and pastoral roles. Whether you or someone you know keeps churchgoing at arm's length, it is important to remember that there are a lot of good and wonderful people to meet there, not to mention a loving God who cares. Our hope is that you will find healing for old wounds and not give up finding a church home where you do feel safe and know you belong.

In addition, when someone is self-employed, it's easy to make your church home a place for networking and promoting your business. While it's not wrong for people there to ask for your services, it's tempting to compromise and alter our motives from the spiritual—loving God and His people—to the transactional—what we can gain from the people we meet.

It's also important to remember that the pain caused by even one person's actions at church can run so deep, it's almost impossible to recover on your own strength and will-power. Forgiveness is key, but it sometimes seems impossible to do by yourself. For Tricia, she needed years of counseling and heartache before she came to the point of forgiveness. And when she did, she taught us a lot about doing the same. Strength comes in numbers, so it's best to reach out to some-one you trust for their help, insight, and, at the very least, the compassion and comfort that come from knowing you're not alone—preferably someone who's mature and has been around the block a few more times than you.

QUESTIONS FOR TRANSFORMATION——————

- If you've got church hurt of any kind, will you consider any offense with the person (or people) involved and separate it from the church body as a whole? This will remove the cloud of hurt from the institution and place it on the indi-vidual(s). Also, are you able to talk openly with your spouse about anyone who has hurt you in your church experience?

- Have you gone directly to the person (or people) who have hurt you to talk with them about it? Matthew 18:15 says, "If your brother or sister sins, go and point out their fault, just between the two of you. If they listen to you, you have won them over." If possible and appropriate, will you consider applying this truth to your own situation? There are times when someone who's hurt you isn't even aware.

- Will you consider taking steps toward forgiveness? Doing so will release you from the grip that pain can have on your heart and usher you into the healing that's needed for full recovery.

- Do you know someone who avoids church because of a hurtful experience? Will you take extra steps to minister to them in their pain and be an influence for their return?
- Transitioning now from church hurt to someone closer, do you have any unforgiveness in your heart toward your spouse? Do you realize that any unforgiveness you harbor takes away your freedom?

11

Searching . . . and a Moment of Truth

One thing we all think we need in life is happiness, so when we don't find it, it's natural to be on the lookout for what will bring it. Up to now, I'd looked for it in Tim, but hadn't found it. So then I looked for it in other men, and still didn't find it. But then people who were close to me continually steered me toward finding it in myself. It was a constant message I'd heard over the years: "Kathy, you need to find yourself—that is the key."

But how does one do that? How do you "find yourself," and how do you know you've actually done it? I didn't know the answers, I just knew I had a longing for more and an inner drive to keep searching for whatever it was I needed. Way back shortly after Tricia was born, my mom and I had both earned our GEDs together—she hadn't graduated from high school either. And over the years since then, I'd taken some college courses, gone to counselors, and then got very heavy into working out and focusing on my body and what I looked like. I even tried to read the Bible, but I'd get as far as the middle of Genesis and stop. Nothing really *satisfied my longing. So when one of my best friends since high school and I were talking on the phone, and she asked if I'd ever heard of Landmark Forum, my interest was piqued.*

"Kathy, my sister went to it, and it was a life changer for her. Now I'm going, so you should go with me!"

In Case You Were Wondering . . .
KATHY

This season in my life I was very obsessed with what my body looked like. I worked out to the extreme. I had gotten breast implants and I liked the way other men looked at me. Tim and I went to Mexico a lot, so looking good in a bikini was very important to me. Inside I was empty, so when the opportunity came to try something new, I didn't even question it. Maybe the Landmark Forum would be the answer. I was all in. I would try anything to fill the void, and once again, I would work it around a boyfriend for a moment of happiness. My search continued.

I trusted her and was definitely in a place where I needed life to change, so I decided on the spot to go. The kids were older, and I finally had the time and freedom to explore what it meant to find myself once and for all. I was open to anything, and since the conference was across the state in Seattle, Tim wouldn't be there looking over my shoulder for three whole days. It also intrigued me that I had a "sort of" boyfriend who lived nearby, so it would be a good opportunity to meet with him—at least that's what I thought. But after I arrived and attended the Friday night session, I realized that hooking up with another guy was not part of

reaso reaso

the plan. I felt strongly that I needed to be fully engaged—I needed to focus only on me. So that's what I did.

Once I got into the Saturday session, I was so excited by what I was learning, I called Tim on my breaks and started talking and sharing what I'd learned. Before then, I didn't talk much at all in our marriage, so what few things I'd learned already were making a very big difference. I was able to simply talk to Tim, share my feelings, share about me from my heart. I even told him about the guy I had planned on hooking up with and was prepared for the consequences. It was as though a wellspring had opened, and there was no closing it, and it felt good.

When Kathy said she wanted to go to Landmark Forum, I remember thinking, "Hey, I can spend the weekend with my girlfriend while Kathy is away." I even knew my girlfriend's ex-husband would have their kids, so that meant more time together with her. I was so messed up in my thinking, I actually wondered how I could have two wives in the same house! So, after she left for Seattle, I spent that Friday night with my girlfriend, and on Saturday, Kathy started calling me on her breaks—she had so much to talk about. I couldn't believe the change in her in such a short time. That night, after spending the evening with my girlfriend, I went home late, got on the phone again with Kathy, and talked with her until after one o'clock in the morning. Kathy seemed so different. We could talk all night like when we first dated. She said she wanted me to come up to attend the Sunday evening session with her, but when I told my girlfriend, she said that if I left, she was done with me—she said it was time to choose, and that she wanted me to choose her; she had divorced her husband. That wasn't what I wanted to hear. She was dear to me and I loved her, but I felt such a strong need to see what Kathy was talking about—there was something so different about her—so I chose her. I flew to Seattle thinking the relationship with my girlfriend was over.

When I got there and saw Kathy, I couldn't *believe* the difference—she looked stunning to me. Her look, her demeanor, just everything about her was different. After attending the final session together, we drove all night to get home. Now, normally when Kathy rode in the car with me, she'd sleep. But that night, she talked, and talked, and talked all the way home. She was so beautiful in a different way, and I loved it. It felt as though the seminar and our time together were huge building blocks for us to grow closer.

When we got home, I thought, *Well, I'll do this too—I'll go to a seminar myself and see what happens for me.* There was one the following May closer to us in Spokane, so I signed up right away. In the meantime, it only took a few days before I got one phone call from my girlfriend for me to go back to her—the tie was just too strong. It was quite the situation because I thought I was in love with two different women, and I couldn't find it in me to stop.

In Case You Were Wondering . . .
TIM

Seeing Kathy at the forum was like seeing her for the very first time, only better. Going through the forum myself made me understand that a couple things were holding us back. In my mind, I only needed to share my current situation and then a past one that I knew would really hurt, but the others were normal guy stuff that I would just keep inside.

Life after the forum was amazing. I felt myself falling deeper in love with Tim than ever—I even discussed having another baby with him. My confidence was like it had never been before. By the time Tim's conference came, I had taken steps to get more involved in his world of the car business to get closer to him and signed up to attend a car sales training course in Chicago with Tricia. At age eighteen, she was working with us in the business by then, and it worked out perfectly to go while Tim was away. I had high expectations for him because of how much it had changed my life—I felt sure he'd come home with a lot to talk about just as I had. Only he didn't wait until he got home. He called me from the conference, and, while I knew he'd have some things to share, I wasn't quite prepared for what he had to say . . .

Thoughts from the Kids . . .
TJ

When Mom came back from the forum, I told my girl-friend, now wife, my mom had gone crazy. She was different, but I didn't understand why, like she went away and got hypnotized or something. Later, after mom and dad both went, they sent us kids. It was a great experience, but as a seventeen-year-old, I didn't quite have the baggage in life that most people carry when they're older. Ultimately, I know it was all part of Mom and Dad's healing process. But man, I still thought Mom was a little crazy at the time.

When I left for the forum, I felt such a sense of peace. There was no Kathy; there was no girlfriend; it was just me to focus on. I felt something working in me, preparing me to get cleaned up. I quickly realized from what I began to learn at the conference that the affair I'd been having was holding me back. I gained enough confidence to fully believe that I didn't need a girlfriend. I felt a new, strong need deep down to tell the *truth*, at least about my current behavior, not about past matters. But it was a start.

I called my girlfriend and told her I was going to tell everything about us to Kathy, and that we had to stop. I said, "You told me to choose, so I'm choosing Kathy once and for all. I need to do this."

Then I dialed Kathy's number, and when she picked up, I said, "Kathy, I have something I need to tell you, and you're not going to like it. I have been having an affair with another woman. You know her, and I will tell you anything you want to know about it when we both get home." In my mind I thought I could share about this one affair but nothing more.

One of the biggest things I learned at the forum was this: You're always choosing the life you want. It's like a vanilla or chocolate kind of choice. Choose what you want for your life and move forward with it in the choice you make. Between this new mindset and my upbringing in the church, I knew my response to Tim's confession mattered. But first, I let myself get mad. I mean really *mad.*

As Tricia and I flew home, I proceeded to get drunk. This way I could drown out the pain I was feeling from the news Tim had dumped in my lap. And things weren't very pretty for a while after I got home. I had a lot of anger and hurt that took some time to talk through and process. If not for the new tools I had learned at Landmark, I think my response would have been different, because I eventually calmed down and knew that I needed to forgive Tim. After all, he'd forgiven me for all my indiscretions—now it was my turn. And I didn't stop there. I even went on to forgive his girlfriend. A few days later, I actually called to tell her I forgave her and even apologized for the hurt and damage Tim had caused in her life. After all, she left her husband while hoping for him. But I didn't even stop there. I told her about the forum and asked her to go, and she did! It was truly amazing.

Of course, I didn't realize that while Tim had confessed to what ended up being two betrayals, he wasn't giving full disclosure—there were so many more acts he was keeping from me. And neither one of us understood or recognized just how God would get his attention to work them out once and for all.

Thoughts from the Kids . . .
TRICIA

I was with my mom when my dad confessed his affair. In the time leading up to the confession I had my suspicions. I was good friends with the woman my dad was having an affair with, and certain things just didn't make sense. So, on one side, I had my mom, whom I was close to and who was hurting. On the other side, I had my friend who was also hurting. Then there was me in the middle of it all, dealing with the fallout and the betrayal from my friend and my dad. I, of course, chose my mom in this situation but it wasn't without lots of hurt and drama. Because I witnessed so much pain and trauma from my parents' affairs, I went into my marriage believing that the key to a successful marriage was to never have infidelity. In fact, I put a stake in the ground and said that would not happen. While this is extremely helpful, my husband and I have learned that there is much more to it than that. We have a strong marriage, but simply not cheating doesn't automatically give you the perfect marriage. It goes a long way, but there is much more to it than that.

Thoughts from the Kids . . .
TJ

Infidelity was kind of something I was raised with as a teenager to be normal—so much so, there was some in the first years of my marriage. Not only was my dad my cheerleader, but he was typically the one that springboarded most of it. I'm not blaming him, as I was responsible for my own decisions. It was 100 percent on me. However, looking back, what kind of dad, who I know loves my wife with his whole heart, would be okay with his behavior influencing me that way? Once again, I don't blame him—it's on me, and the experience ultimately ended up changing my thoughts about it and life forever.

I remember when I first met my wife, she came to a company event my dad's company was putting on. As I kind of pointed people out in the room and who they were, I said, "That's the GM, that's the office manager, and that's my dad's girlfriend. Amanda was like, "Wait what?" It wasn't public knowledge at this time, but I knew what was going on. I think I was trying to be funny, but Amanda didn't think it was very funny.

WHAT ABOUT YOU?

When we do something behind our spouse's back, then try to withhold it from them, there will always be a barrier preventing full and true connection, not to mention broken trust. The bottom line is, being truthful, giving full disclosure is vital for having a strong marriage. This is something that took us decades to learn. Don't wait like we did. Telling the truth—getting matters out in the open—gives marriages more of a chance for restoration and growth. It also lifts the heavy weight that comes with harboring a secret. Telling Kathy the things I'd done was the right and freeing thing to do, yet holding the prior things back kept me in bondage. The burdens I carried were a lot of what led to thinking of taking my life. I'll talk more about this in chapter 15.

If this is speaking to you now, depending on how hurtful an offense may be, remember that appropriate timing and sometimes even professional guidance is okay, even helpful. The important thing is to do whatever possible to set you both up for rebuilding trust and healing.

QUESTIONS FOR TRANSFORMATION————

- Do you have something you've not shared with your spouse that could be keeping you from the intimacy you so want? Consider the full scope of this question. It could be a one-night indiscretion, long-term behavior, or even something you've done or do online or on your phone. The truth will set you free, as we've been sharing the last several chapters. These walls need to be broken down to have a truly successful and close marriage.

- If there is something and you're ready to get it out in the open, will you carefully consider the best way to share it—the two of you alone, or maybe with a counselor—then have the courage to do so?
- On the flip side, if you are on the receiving end of hearing your spouse's confession, will you listen with a heart of grace and forgiveness? It's so important to be thankful when secrets are exposed—even when it hurts. We know it's easier said than done, but it is possible. It's only then that true healing can take place.

12

Winds of Change

By the beginning of 2002, life began to bring on some new beginnings in different ways for the Bush family. We continued to work on our marriage the best we knew how, and while we were still drinking, we were also trying to get healthy. We also made the decision to try and simplify our life by downsizing from the 4,500-square-foot home where we raised the kids into a 2,400-square-foot condo on the Columbia River, and by June, Tim, Blake, and I had all moved into the condo. In February 2003 our middle son, TJ—then eighteen—married Amanda, and only six months later our daughter Tricia married Jimmy. That came with our first grandson, James, and in the fall of 2004, Trey was born. Then six months later Gavin came. So there was a lot of change in our family for such young grandparents. At the same time, we were still trying to figure ourselves out.

Not long after, Tim got the idea to develop more condos on the property along the river called Riverwalk. He also ran a Suzuki car dealership he'd started in early 1999, without my support. For the next couple of years, we adjusted to our changes, and it was during this time that I got the bug to pursue my interest in skin care. My dream was to go to aesthetic school, but there wasn't one close enough to home—I couldn't leave because Blake was still in school—so I went to a local beauty school with the thought of attending a very fine aesthetic school the next year after he graduated. At the local school I attended for a few months, as hard as I tried to make it work, I dropped out. After being a high school dropout and then a beauty school dropout, this was not good for my self-esteem.

In the winter of 2004, Tim's Pop got sick, which brought Tim to a surprising crossroad of reconciliation with his brother Ned. They had hardly spoken for over a decade, so reconnecting with him came as a complete surprise.

Yeah, by right after Thanksgiving my Pop got sick, and Ned took him to the hospital. I was so thankful he was there to help Pop, and I, of course, wanted to see Pop as much as I could. I took our motor home to Vancouver and left it at an RV park, so I'd have a place to stay whenever I visited. For a few months, I drove down to see him at the hospital where I also saw Ned—he was visiting too. Before then, we had spoken very little for thirteen or fourteen years because of a disagreement Gram had discussed between us, not with both of us at the same time, and we each had our own twisted version.

One day when I was there, Ned and I had lunch together, and he shared his disappointment about some decisions I'd made in the past. As we talked more, he finally said with a little trepidation, "Hey, I gotta ask you about something Gram said years ago." As he repeated what she'd said, I pushed back a little saying that that wasn't how things went. After I told him what really happened, we both began to realize our ill feelings over all these years were based on a miscommunication from

Gram—what she'd said to each of us wasn't entirely accurate. We'd literally lived with no relationship at all because of a misunderstanding that neither of us took steps to try and clarify from the start. It was a bit mind-blowing for us both. Shortly after that discovery, Pop died, so I was glad Ned and I had reunited through such an otherwise difficult time. It helped us both during our sad time of loss.

Ned's and my renewed relationship continued, and later that spring, he and his wife, Kate, and daughter, Mady, were visiting Kathy and me. At one point while Ned and I were sitting outside talking, he said, "You know, I've always wanted to open a coffee shop, but I'm trying to figure out how to do it." I said, "Why don't you move here and open one!" So he did. He went home and bought one of those coffee trailer kiosks, hauled it to Tri-Cities, and parked it in the back of our dealership in the shop. Within the next ninety days or so, he and Kate sold their home and moved near us.

At the same time, Kathy was dreaming of going to aesthetic school and looking at her options, and by that summer, she decided to go to the Euro Institute in Renton, Washington, from August through the following March, so eight-and-a-half months she'd be away. My mind went into kind of a panic mode, and I decided to build Kathy her dream condo. Only problem was, it wasn't her dream.

Honestly, I was afraid that if she went to the school and graduated, she wouldn't come home. I figured she'd "find herself" in her new certification, new skills, and a newfound confidence to go out on her own. In other words, she wouldn't need me anymore, but my survival mode needed her to need me. So I did whatever I could to make her want to return, and in my mind, a brand-new condo decked out with anything she wanted should do it. I even told her I'd retire, and we could travel together in our new motor home. But she wasn't impressed or open to changing her mind. So I relented and said, "Okay, let's just take the new motor home to Renton and set it up for you." And that's what we did.

Before she left, I set Kathy up with an interior designer to go over all the features she wanted in the new condo while she packed her stuff, and then she left. I sold the current condo we were in and moved in with TJ and Amanda and their son, Trey, our grandson, while building the new place. The plan was to have it completed by the time Kathy graduated the following March. It was also a time when I was finally being faithful to her.

Planning for school was surreal for me because I had never been on my own. Remember, I had gone straight from living with my parents to marrying Tim. I had so many thoughts in my head. I was ready to move out and get away from Tim. I thought that being away from him might give me some real time to evaluate what life without kids was going to look like in my future. Would I develop a skill that would get me a job so I could support myself? What would my life look like without Tim's control? Would I even want to come back to him once school was done?

Once I arrived, I knew from the first day of school that I was right where I needed to be. I felt that as the teacher spoke to the whole class, she was speaking directly to me. I knew in my heart God wanted me there—I just got that sense. I had been searching for who I was, and I knew that at that school I would find out, and I was so excited.

Later that day, a man I had been having an affair with came over to see me, but my focus on school and all I would learn was

my priority. I made it clear to him I was giving my all to my stud-
ies, and there was no room for him in my life. And that was the
end of him. At the same time, I knew Tim really missed me, but I
even made it clear to him that if he wanted to come visit, he would
have to help me study.

Well, he was a trooper and respected my boundaries. He
didn't come often, but when he did, he was very helpful. He lis-
tened and learned all about skin right along with me and was
willing to be my first guinea pig to give a facial.

I not only loved every minute of school, but I was surprised
by how well I did—I got straight A's. I hardly ever drank, and
I tried to soak in all I could learn and apply myself as much as
possible. It felt great. In my past, I didn't ever do well in a school
environment, yet this time I loved it.

But as graduation drew near, I began to feel the dread of
returning to Tim and losing the freedom I had while being on
my own. It made me want to party and sow my oats before
returning to the real world with him again. I imagine it was
how kids feel in college as they approach graduation, and they
want to party before they have to get back to reality. So that's
what I did.

About four weeks before graduation, a few other women and
I decided to take a break from our studying and go for a drink.
That decision was the beginning of losing control of myself again
as I had before—the drinking and smoking marijuana . . . and
men. I still studied hard during the week, but the weekends were
my time of downward spiraling into partying again. And when
I didn't answer Tim's calls in the early morning hours, he called
more and came on even stronger. I felt as though I was going back
into a cage.

In Case You Were Wondering . . .
TIM

I drove a late model Crown Victoria or Lincoln each visit I made to see Kathy. I played tunes and sang at the top of my lungs and cried uncontrollably the entire drive home. My heart was broken. My grief of losing Pop was still stirring, and now it felt like I was losing Kathy.

By then, Kathy stopped answering my calls at midnight, then one o'clock, two o'clock, three and four, and I was afraid something was up. The next day she'd finally pick up and say she'd been asleep—and I wanted to believe her. I just knew I was anxious for school to be over so I could fly up to Seattle, pick her up, and bring her to our new home.

When that day finally came, it was like seeing her after the Landmark Forum all over again. She looked *beautiful* to me! She literally hugged and kissed me like she really wanted me, and boy was I relieved. What was really exciting was her news about graduation day. I couldn't have felt prouder.

There were about twenty other women who completed the program, and that day was filled with an extra buzz of energy. I went with a friend and bought a new outfit and even got my makeup done at Nordstrom—it was a very special day in my life. By the time we were all seated and the ceremony began, the instructor talked about the accomplishments of all the students, but she eventually began to talk about one student in particular. She spoke about how this woman excelled in her grades, had perfect attendance, and had the highest record of product sales.

At our school's
Homecoming dance,
1981

Celebrating our engagement

Our wedding, February 5, 1982

Our
wedding

Our
honeymoon

Tricia's
baptism

The truck we drove to Roswell, New Mexico

The Dodge Dart we got from selling the big truck

TJ's baptism

Blake's baptism

Blake, Tim, and Pop

Our family
at church

The two of us at the Suzuki grand opening

James, Blake, TJ, and Luke

On one of our many trips to Mexico

The BMW dealership

The plaque at the BMW dealership honoring Luke

Tim, Ned, and Ned's sister

As she spoke, I kept looking at another woman whom I was so impressed with. I had bragged about her to Tim and knew without a doubt the instructor was talking about her. She was going to be the honor student! Only, the instructor said something that took me by surprise. She said this student drove over and stayed in a motor home the entire eight months of classes. But wait, that was me! I couldn't believe it—she was talking about ME! I was shocked. I knew I'd done well in all of the courses, but I didn't think I'd be at the top of the class. It's an amazing moment for me to this day.

Even with such a great accomplishment, I was plagued with the other news I had to tell Tim. The previous fall when I left for school, I didn't know if I wanted to return home, but after my downfall, I knew I wanted to go home, I wanted to be married to him, I felt bad for what I'd done, I felt sick for what I would have to tell him. And I hoped with my heart that he'd forgive me . . . again.

In Case You Were Wondering . . .
KATHY

Going away to school was one of the most exciting things I had ever done. I would finally be out on my own. Would I come back to Tim and the new grandkids? I didn't know, I just thought "Here I am, a grown woman, and I'm still not happy or satisfied. But what is it I am searching for?" That school experience was one of my great accomplishments and one of great regret. How I hurt my husband was a hurt that lasted many years—a hurt that would soon take us to the bottom of our marriage.

WHAT ABOUT YOU?

Several things come to mind in this part of our story. First, thinking back on the years I lost with Ned, all because of a miscommunication, still makes me a bit sick. Our miscommunication involved a third party, so we relied on indirect information, which is not wise. To make matters worse, neither of us made an effort to make amends. We just accepted the situation instead of taking time or focus to clear things up. But this brings me to communication between a husband and a wife. It's so easy to misunderstand something and let it stew rather than make it a point to gain clarity or even a new perspective on what the other person said. Can you relate?

Looking back, how I wish I'd been more proactive about reaching out to Ned rather than losing years of memories we could have had together. If this scenario hits close to home for you, we hope you'll sincerely consider not settling or accepting the situation, but instead take steps toward reconciliation.

Then, new seasons in life will inevitably bring opportunities for new experiences and development, which in turn bring change. And change can be unsettling, a little frightening for a husband or a wife, even when the change is good. We tried to go through our changes on our own, not looking for much help unless the help rang our bells at the same time. We were stubborn. Times like this make good communication, even reassurance, a top priority, not to mention a heart that is glad for the other person's growth.

QUESTIONS FOR TRANSFORMATION————————

- Can you think of a miscommunication between you and your spouse that caused conflict, even a prolonged distance? Perhaps you're nodding your head because you're experiencing one right now. Will you not give up, or simply accept living with ill feelings? Will you take steps to own the solution? Will you humble yourself enough to reach out and ask forgiveness for your part? Time is so valuable; will you press in to set yourselves up for time together rather than apart?

- When your spouse works to achieve a goal or reach a milestone in their life, are you able and willing to share in their journey and back them up? Having some anxiety with change can be normal. Will you be honest and communicate any thoughts that have you feeling unsettled? The point is to walk through change together with a spirit of support and encouragement.

- Is there another relationship—a third party—that could be causing separation or dissention between you and your spouse? Will you talk about the possibility of this and take action to change that relationship to protect your own? Don't lose years of life like Ned and I did. You never know how many years are left.

13

The Bridge

I had no idea about the heartbreaking news Kathy was about to share—I just remember being glad she was coming home and that she made honor student. So my excitement quickly sank when I heard the words, "Tim, I have something to tell you"—a phrase I was all too familiar with. She told me part of what happened before we even left the school, then the rest on the drive home.

When she finished, it hurt like no other time before, but she seemed sincerely sorry and kept saying she wanted to be married to me. Of all her confessions, this one was the most painful because I made the mistake of asking for every detail. To this day I wish I hadn't pressed so hard. It took a decade or so to come to grips with what she shared. She said she was ready to be home and wanted to work things out with us, and this time I could tell she meant it. It felt so cleansing in a way and I thought, *Finally, I think we can move forward*, because I knew I was in a place where I wasn't going to have any other relationships—I was going to be faithful to Kathy. At the same time, working with Ned was going well and we were in good shape financially. Kathy and I had something new to build on.

Or so I thought.

It was only two weeks later when I started to leave for work, went back into the house to give Kathy a goodbye kiss, and caught her on the phone with an old boyfriend (as discussed in chapter 1). When that happened, I was at the point of giving up and wanting a divorce. She wasn't; she wanted to get help—*again*. I reluctantly agreed to see the husband-and-wife counseling team she talked about, but I wanted to fix her *once and for all*.

In Case You Were Wondering . . .
KATHY

This was a rock bottom moment for me. For the first time in our marriage Tim was done. I remember the feeling of desperation as I begged him to stay. Why did I want this marriage to work? Something inside me didn't want to give up. There was not one day we were both willing to give up at the same time, and to this day I'm beyond grateful for that.

Jake and Jennifer agreed to see us fairly quickly, so we got started right away, each individually—Kathy with Jennifer and me with Jake—and then all four of us together. We had faith in them because Jennifer had counseled Tricia for several years to help her through the abuse she had experienced with a church leader.

When I met with Jennifer, I was at a point where I really wanted to be healthy. I wanted to understand why I did the things I did so I could change and heal permanently, not just have a quick fix. So I told her everything—I held nothing back. And as I talked more with her, Tim and I talked through things together at home. I assumed Tim was doing the same thing with Jake—confessing everything. I didn't know he was holding back from sharing all of his indiscretions, which I still didn't know about. The focus was always on me.

Kathy's right. I talked about my life with Jake, especially the abuse I had experienced from Ned's dad, but I didn't share with him any of my unfaithfulness toward Kathy. I justified that decision by thinking that most of the men I knew fooled around—it was normal. Plus, after I married Kathy, someone I highly respected said to let sleeping dogs lie—you don't talk about those things. You take them to the grave. And believe it or not, I didn't want to hurt anybody, and I knew it would hurt Kathy if she found out, so I didn't even go there in my counseling. In my mind, I was doing this to fix her, not me.

As we were counseling, I got a job at a spa to provide skin care—it felt good to begin applying the things I'd learned in school—only I found out I didn't like working for someone else. After completing aesthetic school, I had my own ideas about how to run a business and I was ready to branch out on my own, so in January of 2007, that's what I did. The thing is, I needed a shop location and money to buy equipment and products. Well, Tim and his partners had developed a commercial building on Riverwalk by then, so I worked out a deal with them for a corner spot. At the same time, something good came out of another not-so-good event that happened back while I was at school.

A few weeks before graduation, someone broke into the motor home and stole all of my jewelry, so Tim and I filed an insurance claim that ended up paying out about $26,000! And it was when they finally paid us that I was in the position of wanting to open my own place. My thought was, it was my money. I didn't care about getting a new wedding ring—a simple band was fine with me—and I didn't care about getting new jewelry as much as opening my own business. So I used all of the money for the business and called it Riverwalk European Skin Care. It was so exciting for me and, looking back, I had really come a long way from the quiet, shy girl several decades before whose only motivation was to get married and have a man take care of her.

When all of this was going on, Ned was still working for Tim, and I was excited to see them building a relationship. At the same time, our fourth grandchild named Shane arrived, and soon to follow came Carter.

Ned seemed like such a good man to me. He told me he had joined a men's group that read and studied the Bible and held each other accountable—he literally witnessed to me. I can only say this now as I didn't know what *witnessing* was then. But even though I thought he was good, I wasn't too receptive because, hey, my mindset was that I was a higher-level Christian, and maybe someday Ned would be as good as me! Besides, I didn't need to read the Bible; our pastor read it to us in church. How arrogant was that?! But when Easter Sunday arrived, Kathy and I accepted his invitation to go to his church. It wasn't Lutheran, but we weren't attending regularly anyway, and we didn't realize how different the service would be.

It was a big church compared to what we were used to, and it was filled to the max with people. In the middle of the stage area, they had an actual bridge set up. The pastor spoke well, but he talked in a way we'd not heard before. We now know it was the gospel message of Jesus, only with a different approach than we were used to. He actually said you could have a personal relationship with Jesus! When he finished, he invited people to come forward and walk across the bridge into a new relationship with the Lord. But oh no, there was no way I was going forward—all of it was short of being weird to me.

In Case You Were Wondering . . .
TIM

Going to Bethel in 2007 for me was 100 percent to appease my brother and not any place I was interested in. When walking in that huge place, seeing how it was packed, seeing the bridge, I thought, "What a show." Looking around, all I saw was a bunch of perfect people who were more than likely all hypocrites. There was nothing there for me.

That bridge—seeing it, being asked to walk across it, and accepting Jesus—made a very big impression on my heart that day. I listened to the message and then the invitation, and all I remember was my heart racing. It kept beating so fast because I wanted to do it! I wanted to walk across it! I couldn't understand what was happening because I thought, Wait, I'm already a Christian, so why do I need to walk across that bridge? Why do I even feel such an urgency to get up and go? I already believe in God and that I'm good. *All of this kept going through my head.*

I wrestled and fought with my urge to get up, and the pull to stay seated won. And it was for one reason alone: I was afraid of what Tim would say. He would have embarrassed me by saying, "What are you doing, *Kathy?! Sit down!" So I didn't do it, but I really, really wanted to.*

Later when Ned was over at the house and we were talking about the service, I told him I wanted to stand up and go, and Ned said he did too, but he was afraid. We were both disappointed that we didn't.

Tim, on the other hand, had a much different experience . . .

While the pastor is now a dear friend of mine, that day I just saw a bald guy up there delivering a message while I was thinking, *There are a lot of people in this room!* It was a large sanctuary that held close to 1,500 people, and it was packed. I was more focused on my watch and what time it was, thinking we'd need to get to the nearest exit quickly so we could get out and make it to brunch before everyone else did. *And* get a drink!

Little did I know it was one more time when the Lord was pursuing us, and He definitely made some progress with Kathy. Me? I still had to take another fall with some very hard hits before He'd get my full attention. *And boy, did He.*

WHAT ABOUT YOU?

Counseling.

When this word comes up, it can usher in a lot of emotions for a lot of reasons. Kathy and I certainly spent a lot of time in "the chair." We had reoccurring problems—or a cycle, as Kathy mentioned—and we didn't know how to get out of it. While not all of the counseling we received helped, a lot of it did. Two things, though, about how effective counseling can help:

1. Decide to go to fix *yourself*, not the other person. As much as we'd like to change our spouse, we can't; we can only work on ourselves. When we do, change will eventually come about because of the difference we've made in ourselves. Then,

2. Determine to give full disclosure. Unless you are brutally honest so the counselor has your full picture, their help will remain limited. Kathy did just that—she disclosed everything and wanted to understand her own behavior so she could change it for the long-term. I held back for a long time and remained a prisoner of my secrets. My chains were holding back the life I so desired.

QUESTIONS FOR TRANSFORMATION———

- Is the thought of counseling something you're open to, or do you shun the idea? On that note, can either of you recognize and discuss any reoccurring problem areas you just can't seem to overcome? Is this something you'll look at and discuss with each other? Will you consider all of your options for addressing them? Counseling can be very helpful for getting an outside perspective and learning new ways of addressing issues that you struggle to resolve on your own.

- Do you know there is a difference between believing in God and being a believer? This is something that took me over forty-seven years to figure out. Once I did, I haven't looked back and if you do, neither will you!

- After answering honestly that last question, have you heard a still small voice prompting you to give your life to Jesus? If so, what is holding you back from accepting Him? Pride? Fear? A person? Will you talk with each other candidly about this?

14

The Final Descent

An old favorite board game I used to play is Monopoly. If you haven't played, it's a strategic yet entertaining game about buying, selling, and renting properties, along with the rewards and pitfalls that come with it. While it's only a game, playing it resonated with my own personal drive to emulate the concept into a real-life vision. From the time I was a young man, Pop taught me how to buy and sell property, so I caught the bug early on. My magazine of choice became his last month's multiple listings (MLS) book. I purchased my first house three months after my eighteenth birthday, with plans for another soon after. And over the years, that bug turned into a dream of building my own "kingdom"—and I was getting close to realizing it.

At forty-five years old, my goal was to build and own one hundred properties in ten years' time to develop commercial and residential buildings. Included, of course, were car dealerships, condos, and businesses in the Tri-Cities area of eastern Washington, where Kathy and I lived. I'd buy blocks and rows of property with plans of building on them and renting them out, just like you do in the game . . . only it wasn't a game—it was my revelation, my lifeblood. I was still counseling with Jake, and he called what I did "survival." Because of the hardships I faced growing up, I lived in constant survival mode. In my mind, I would never be good enough; I would never have enough; I would never do enough to feel as though I could stop. As long as I kept my hand to the plow, I'd be okay.

By October of 2007, I had bought enough land for Ned and me to start building. The kingdom in my mind was becoming a reality, and my plan was that, as we got further into the development, I'd make Ned a partner.

But by June of the next year, the progress he and I were making came to a halt—it was something neither of us saw coming. I happened to be watching him from my upstairs office at the used car lot and noticed he had developed a limp. I called his phone to ask about it, but not being a complainer, he brushed it off as a funny little thing. It just didn't seem right, though. A few days later he told me his left hand kept falling off the computer keyboard and he didn't know why, and I told him he really needed to get checked out. He still refused. Then while driving with his daughter, who was around six, his leg went numb, and his foot came off the pedal. So finally, he went to the doctor. At the same time, when all of this was happening, our youngest son Blake got married. It was odd to have such a happy time mixed with the concern we had for what was going on with Ned.

After Ned got tested, the doctor's initial diagnosis was a mass in the back of his head that could be multiple sclerosis, but they wanted to do a biopsy which meant drilling into his brain. Not only was it risky, but Ned kept seeing himself as young and healthy and didn't want to do it. Between his wife, Kate, and me, we convinced him to get it done, and unfortunately, the diagnosis wasn't good. It's a day and a conversation I'll never forget.

Kathy was on a trip for aesthetics in Istanbul, Turkey, so Kate and I went with Ned to the neurosurgeon's office to hear the results. Kate sat on one side, Ned was in the middle, and I sat on the other as he said, "I don't know any other way to tell you than just to tell you, Ned. You need to get your affairs in order; you have stage four glioblastoma, an aggressive form of brain cancer that in most cases won't respond to treatment. You have anywhere from six months to two years to live."

I was *shocked*. Things were not going as I had planned. Ned, only forty-three at the time, was the only brother I had, and we had become so close. I thought, *This can't be*, but it was. He had been talking to me more about God and the Bible, so where was God now? As I tried to process what was happening, the anxiety that continually brewed deep down over the years began to surface again. Between my years of drinking, carousing, keeping my infidelities from Kathy, driving my energy into my work, and now the thought of losing my brother, my mind and body were under attack—again. I was overcome with the thought that I wasn't in control, and I began another downward spiral. Only this time, I had no idea just how far down it would go.

At the same time Tim made progress with growing his kingdom, my business took off and went steadily well. My confidence as a businesswoman grew, and it felt good to fulfill the dream I had worked so hard to reach. It was definitely a season of prosperity for us both—I'd even stopped going to counseling because I had become healthier. Yet the time was very bittersweet on hearing the news about Ned. I could see it weigh on Tim more and more, and eventually I persuaded him to see a naturopath and to reduce his drinking. For quite some time Jake and Jennifer had suggested we both stop drinking—they saw it as the common thread in all of our problems—but we weren't willing to give it up completely. At least not yet.

As the cancer in Ned continued to grow, he continued to press more into God, and by August, his faith led him to get baptized. His story and baptism encouraged several of his friends that weekend to do the same. He even invited me to get baptized, too, but I said no, it wasn't for me. In spite of my resistance, Ned continued to share about God and His Word—he discipled me while I didn't realize that's what he was doing. His seeds of faith continued to bounce off my prideful heart, but that didn't stop him. It didn't stop God, either, from letting me fall even deeper into despair and showing me to an even greater degree just how much I was not in control of life.

After a few months passed, Kathy and I got news that our twenty-two-year-old nephew had taken his life. And at his funeral, I started to get sick with anxiety, only this time it didn't stop. Then just a few days after that, the bank I'd set up loans with for expanding my properties called to say they were going into receivership—there would be no loans. Then just a week before Thanksgiving, Ned went into hospice. By then, I started thinking about and planning to kill myself. I thought it would be easier than dealing with all I was facing and give the family much-needed funds to survive. Honestly, looking back, it was just my selfish manipulation trying to control things one last time.

In Case You Were Wondering . . .
TIM

Pop told me when he passed not to be sad and to be strong for the others. But after all the losses over the past three years, it just wasn't in me anymore to be strong. I'd mentally given up and was ready to be done with life.

Thoughts from the Kids . . .
TJ

Luke's death was one of the worst and most pivotal days in my life. I didn't know this then, but God used Luke's death to bring me to Him. Luke was already a Christian, so as tragic as it was, and still is at times, I know where he is now. God uses these things to get more of us to turn to Him. I never had a "relationship" with the Lord before this. I didn't even know what that meant. However, now I do, and looking back, Luke dying, as much as I miss him, was a huge part of finding God for me.

Thoughts from the Kids . . .
BLAKE

Our family was broken with no one left to hold us together. Even Dad, who would normally be the idea guy or the man to look to for support in terrible situations, had nothing to give. It was like a fog rolled in on our family and there was no light to see even a foot in front of us. Luke was my cousin, my best friend, and I had never experienced loss like that. It was one of the worst experiences I had ever lived through. When Ned passed away, I was already so numb to life with no hopes of ever feeling normal again. This was the beginning of what I know God was doing to bring us all to Him. I have heard from so many people that when you hit rock bottom, you turn to Jesus. This was definitely our rock bottom.

Thoughts from the Kids ...
AMANDA

I was the office manager during this time, and I remember when we got the call from the flooring bank that floored all the vehicle inventory. Flooring fronts your money to buy vehicles, then you pay off the flooring once the car is sold. They were calling for $200k in payoffs. If I remember correctly, it was over $200k, and we didn't have this money because Tim had pulled the money to pay the building payables—the bank that was financing the new dealership would not give him a draw since they were in receivership. They were playing hardball and Tim just didn't show up. Tim's presence was scarce; he later said that he avoided coming into the dealership because I would be able to tell something was up. He would come in and sign checks or leave me notes when he knew I was gone.

One day Kathy called us (me, TJ, and Blake since we all worked at the dealership). We put the call on speaker, and she said, "Dad is really bad. He can't come into work, he can't talk about work, so don't call the house (something to this effect). This was after Luke and Ned had passed, and TJ and Blake could barely hold it together. Now Tim had a no-contact order. So, Tim was out, and Blake (our top salesperson) and TJ (used car manager) were hanging on by threads. Things didn't look or feel good.

I was told by the receptionist to call Uncle Steve. He basically wanted to understand what was going on, sent the money, and basically helped me figure it out. I remember thinking, "I can't do this all on my own, having a baby with me at work, breastfeeding, working, all while watching out for Blake and TJ." She may have not known it at the time, but Kathy was a strong influence on me. I thought, "If she's going to be the rock, then I'll be the rock." That mentality has stayed with me my whole marriage.

I was still seeing Jake and now seeing a holistic doctor, but I was barely hanging on and kept searching for how to be healed. I didn't sleep for what felt like the whole month of December, and I literally felt like I was going crazy. I had to stop working, which was something I'd never experienced before. I was afraid of everything, and claustrophobia set in to the point that I couldn't wear socks. I wouldn't even let Kathy leave me alone by myself—she had to stay with me or I had to go with her to her office. What really got me, though, was that Ned was dying, yet instead of seeing him panic or struggle or fall apart like I was, he had peace. He had calm. He had what I desperately wanted but couldn't have, and I didn't understand it.

By the next month, January of 2009, I was so broken and full of anxiety, I asked Jake if it might be from all the abuse I had suffered under Ned's dad. He thought it could be, so he had me get a big box of toilet paper from Costco, put duct tape all over it so it wouldn't fall apart, and then beat that box with a bat for as long as it took to get all my anger out. So I did. I beat it and cried until I couldn't do it anymore, and I thought that was going to be the end of my suffering. But it wasn't.

Then Jake wondered if there might be something else in my life I had not shared that needed to come out.

"Is there anything you haven't told me, Tim?"

That's when I finally did it. I told him about all my years of infidelities—one by one. I even thought I had a daughter from many years before that I'd never met.

"Tim, this is no small matter. You've been holding in all these secrets from Kathy, and there won't be true healing in you or between the two of you until you tell her. You might lose her, you might not. But I do know you've got to tell her *everything*."

So I did.

———————

As I listened to Tim confess each of his infidelities, I remember saying, "Is that all?" Then he'd tell me about another one, and

I'd say it again, "Is that all?" And for two hours he unloaded all he'd done over the past twenty-seven years of our marriage. I don't remember feeling any anger; I just felt sorry for him. Yes, I hurt, but his anxiety was so bad—he was so miserable—I hurt more for him than I wanted to lash out. And for the first time, the dynamics of our marriage were starting to make sense. I could connect the dots I had not been able to until then. Whenever I confessed to him, I never quite understood his reactions and why he always forgave me. I always wondered why he didn't leave me. I finally realized it was because through all those years, he was guilty of the same things and more, I just didn't know it.

In Case You Were Wondering . . .
KATHY

I'm sure you're wondering how I could stay with Tim after he confessed all his infidelity. Did I stay because I had been unfaithful too? Did I think we were now even? I would learn so much about forgiveness in the coming years, but as for this time, I believe the supernatural power of God is what got me through.

I believe the timing of Tim telling me about his cheating was in God's plan, too, because Tim was in such bad shape both mentally and physically, I honestly didn't know if he was going to live. So my hurt for him overshadowed any anger I probably should have had.

Then, on February 28, 2009, after just a few short weeks of processing it all, Ned passed away.

WHAT ABOUT YOU?

It is only natural to wake up each morning and think we're in control of our lives. We are, to some degree, when it comes to daily activities and the decisions we make. But in the bigger picture, we have little control when disaster hits and throws us completely off the course we've planned. Sickness, death, financial loss, the effects of someone else's choices on our own lives—all these factors can shake our very foundation. And when that happens, we can react in ways we never thought possible—we just do whatever we think will bring an end to our pain and suffering. Which leads us to the subject of suicidal thoughts . . .

Suicide and its lure for being the answer to any dilemma is very real and very much the wrong answer to any problem. It's actually a selfish answer, because while taking your own life removes you from the equation, it leaves even more burden and lasting pain on those you love. It's hard to look back at what I almost did to my family. *Every* problem has a solution, so it's important to choose not to give up hope.

Can you relate? We all have tragedy hit at some time or another—no one is immune. It is our hope that you remember there is always hope, always an end that leads to brighter days.

QUESTIONS FOR TRANSFORMATION————

- As we said, no one is immune to the tragedies life can bring; it's what we do in their wake that matters. Perhaps you're in one right now and don't know where to turn. Will you be honest with yourself and your spouse if you've ever had—or may have now—thoughts of suicide? Do you struggle with believing the lie that taking your life is a good solution? If so, will you reach out and tell someone? There is *always* help, but you've got to let someone know you need it.

• God's Word says, "At the name of Jesus every knee should bow, in heaven and on earth and under the earth" (Philippians 2:10), and when He took me to my knees, it wasn't a momentary thing—He kept me there for over a year, and yes, it was scary. Have you ever been put on your knees by uncontrollable circumstances? Have you been made to bow to Him because there was nothing left to do? Perhaps you are there now. Or are you not sure you believe this can even happen? Trust me when I say it *can* and *did* happen to me. Nothing could fix me, not even medication. Only total trust in someone I knew nothing about . . . yet.

15

The Lighthouse

The thought of giving the eulogy at Ned's funeral, and then actually doing it, was one of the hardest things I've ever faced—besides telling Kathy all my secrets. It didn't help that my anxiety had reached the point of a friend recommending I see a psychiatrist, which I eventually did. Even after all my confessions to Kathy, I still couldn't get my body to calm down and feel normal.

Work had always been my source of survival, but I couldn't work at that point or even for the next year; the bank was going into receivership, so plans for my kingdom had stopped; family members were dying; mortality was setting in; I was used to solving problems, but I couldn't solve anything. I actually tried to go bankrupt as a solution but couldn't even get approval to do that. I eventually isolated myself from my friends, and as a result, the same rationalization for dealing with everything kept playing in my mind: "Was it time to give up? Maybe I should kill myself." But, looking back, I can see how God didn't let that happen. He continued His pursuit of me in ways I couldn't have thought of or coordinated on my own . . .

———————

It was early March and by a week after Ned's funeral, I was taking medication prescribed by the psychiatrist for bipolar disorder (which turned out to be a misdiagnosis) as well as maximum doses of Xanax, plus I was drinking a fifth of alcohol every day just to try and feel normal. I completely depended on my cocktail regimen, but it still wasn't enough for me to be able to see our new granddaughter.

Tricia, who had been expecting, went into labor twelve weeks early, and Kaylene, our first granddaughter, was born weighing only two pounds seven ounces. She had to stay in the NICU for forty-one days before going home. What made that time especially difficult was that Tim, because of his claustrophobia, couldn't put on the gown or shoe covers required for going into her room, and I couldn't leave Tim. Neither one of us could see or support Tricia or our granddaughter. It was a very hard thing for me to process and accept.

Thoughts from the Kids . . .
TRICIA

On March 13, 2009, Kaylene was born twelve weeks early. This was after six weeks of bed rest. Shortly after she was born, my parents left for Mexico. I didn't know what was going on with my dad at the time, so I had no idea how bad things really were. I only knew they were leaving at a time when we really needed help. We had Shane, a two-year-old, and Gavin, a four-year-old at home with no childcare for Shane. I couldn't believe that they were leaving the country. I remember being so angry and hurt, going to the NICU at three o'clock in the morning and staying till Jimmy had to leave for work. In the evenings, we would get a babysitter and go see Kaylene once he was off work. It was a challenging time.

In the meantime, Kathy and I had been planning to fly to Mexico for a board meeting that was scheduled for a vacation club where we were members. We flew first class, yet as comfortable as that normally is, once they closed the door I was sweating and claustrophobic to the point of not being comfortable in my own skin. I couldn't stand to have shoes on.

Despite the state Tim was in, we arrived okay, and after Tim attended the board meeting, his friend Bob, who was also president of the board, came to me, took me aside, and asked, "Is Tim alright? He's really been working on me to get him some drugs! What should I do?" Well, I caught him up to speed on Tim and told him I was at the point of not knowing what to do. I said, "You may as well get them for him, because he's going to get them one way or another."

Later when I saw Bob, I thought he had brought some drugs for me, only instead of handing me what I asked for, he held out a bottle of valerian root supplements! *Not* what I wanted. He then said, "Listen, Tim, I want you to know I talked to Kathy and know more about what's going on, so I want you to realize that I can still get you some drugs, but I think you should consider something else. Maybe you should consider reading the Bible."

"Bob, I *am*! I read seventy pages a night—the Bible in one hand, whiskey in the other—and I'm not getting anything out of it. I'm freaking out; I'm *sick* here! Something's going on, and I can't help it." Bob said, "Wait . . . Why don't you slow down and read just one chapter of Proverbs a day?"

I didn't even know what Proverbs was or where it was in the Bible—I hadn't gotten that far in my reading yet. But I said I'd think about it.

When we got home, we asked Kathy's parents to come over so we could share what was going on with me. Kathy said we didn't need advice because we were in counseling; we just needed them to listen. She told them I was seeing a psychiatrist and didn't know what else to do. A few weeks later, Kathy's mom came to see me, but I was in no shape to even go downstairs and told Kathy I couldn't, so she talked to Kathy. Her mom knew of most of our terrible marriage story. After she left, Kathy came upstairs and told me, "Mom said that with all you've done, maybe this would be a good time to get out." But my wonderful wife—whom I didn't deserve—said, "Tim, I'm sticking with you no matter what, even if we lose everything." She said she was with me for the long haul.

Looking back at that conversation, I believe it's the first time I ever saw Jesus—I saw Him through Kathy. She gave me unconditional love I didn't deserve and something I trusted like never before. Her mom was right; my old self wasn't worthy of being married to Kathy. Yet God wasn't done with me yet.

A few weeks later, Tim finally came to me and said, "Listen, one thing Bob said to me when we were in Mexico was to read a chapter in Proverbs a day. I'm thinking maybe we should give it try. Do you want to read together?" When Tim asked that question, I was so excited! It was the first time he'd led me in a spiritual way, and I was thrilled. When I think back, I would say it is the sexiest thing Tim has ever done. We started with chapter one and stayed the course, and as we got more into it, we noticed Tim's high anxiety starting to go down little by little. For me, reading God's Word started to make sense for the first time. Not only was I able to understand what I read, I started to feel inspired by it. It was my favorite time of the day.

I was also feeling good inside because it felt like Tim and I were growing closer as we read. It was a turning point because I began to realize it was the first time Tim depended on me. And despite how difficult my new role as his caregiver had been, my love for him changed—my heart softened toward him. He had always taken care of me, and now I was able to care for him. He needed me rather than the other way around. Through it all, I felt I had really stepped up. My new circumstances challenged me and made me grow stronger and more confident, plus all the ways he'd been controlling me had disappeared—he didn't have it in him anymore, and I liked that.

In Case You Were Wondering . . .
TIM

When I told Bob I was reading the Bible, it was out of pure desperation. I was speed reading, hoping I would find answers. When Kathy and I started reading a chapter of Proverbs a day, things started changing. I had no idea what was about to come.

In Case You Were Wondering ...
KATHY

I will repeat this: Tim asking me to read the Bible with him was the sexiest thing to this day he has ever done. Husbands, I hope you hear this loud and clear! Religion versus having a relationship with Christ are so very different. To make Jesus the Lord of your life is different from merely believing in God. Religion was embedded in me, and the only way to break through that was repenting and finally hearing God in his Word. God literally saved me through his Word. Repentance from my former ways and turning toward God was key.

As Kathy and I started reading together, another bright light that shined on me was a pastor named Bill Voris—the one who visited and prayed and took Ned through his death. Bill befriended me and asked if I'd like to join a group to help go through my grief, and I told him he lost me at the word *group*! So he offered to meet me one-on-one, and I said okay.

By April, we started meeting, and I really liked him. He was five-foot-seven and weighed about 140 pounds, which was the same height and weight as my Pop. He even had the same mannerisms and called me Timmer like my Pop, so I had an attraction to him for sentimental reasons. As we met and got to know each other well, one day he looked at me and said, "Tim, I need to talk to you about something, and I need to close the door this time." He got up and closed it. (At this point my claustrophobia had improved enough that I could at least have the door closed.) Then he said, "Tim, I've been a pastor for over forty years, and I've never had a conversation like this with anyone—I could even lose my job—but I think it's from the Lord, and I want you to really listen to me.

"The Lord's got a calling on your life. It's a *big* calling, and it's not here. I think you need to find a Jesus-loving, Bible-teaching church and figure out what your calling is, because it's *not here*." I listened carefully to what he said, and I didn't tell him this, but I didn't know what a "calling" was! But I heard what he said very clearly and took it all in.

I went home and told Kathy what he'd said, and she didn't know what a calling was either, but she said, "Whatever it is, I'm in. Let's go find it!" And she was game-on about finding a Jesus-loving, Bible-teaching church. The thing is, we thought *all* churches were that, so we weren't quite sure what we were looking for, but we went ahead and started our search to find one.

By this time, Tim was on a journey of good health. I had for the most part wished Tim would take his health into his own hands, especially after I finished school. I also wanted to eat well and exercise, so Tim found a company called AdvoCare that offered natural treatment for whole living, and we both got on their products. It required a total digestive cleanse, which meant Tim had to stop drinking for twenty-eight days. Between that, changing his diet, getting on supplements, and us reading the Bible together, we could tell that his anxiety continued to get better.

We also tried new churches and did what we could to figure out what Tim's calling was, and before we knew it, we'd finished reading through Proverbs. By then, we liked it so much, we didn't want to stop, so we decided to keep going and read the Psalms.

Through it all, Tim's anxiety was still there, but the changes we made were helping. I also continued to experience a deeper spiritual presence of God as I read more and more of His Word. I truly felt my life was changing for the good.

By early August, I went to a women's conference held by AdvoCare, and I could tell that the women who spoke were Christians, yet something about them was different. I was used to people talking about God, but these women kept talking about Jesus and the Lord in such a personal way—as though He was close and involved with details of their everyday lives. One of the women I met was from our area in Tri-Cities, so I approached her after the conference and asked, "What church do you go to?" She said, "I go to The Living Room church." That name sounded familiar, and when I thought about it, I remembered that's where our niece attended, and she said it was life-changing for her. When I got home, I told Tim about the church.

Yeah, I also remember our niece saying it was life-changing for her, so we talked about giving it a try. But right then, I was focused on my upcoming thirtieth high school reunion. I was class president and was part of the planning every year. It was always a party, and I was the driver of it. I had rented a suite for the after-party and *loaded* it with alcohol.

Well, we went to the reunion, and we drank. And drank. And drank. And the morning after brought Kathy to a new realization.

When I opened my eyes, I remember so clearly seeing Taco Bell wrappers strewn around the room and thinking, I am so tired of feeling like this; I am so tired of being hung over; I am so tired of wondering what I did last night. I had so many regrets for getting drunk, and Tim and I even talked about how maybe Jake and Jennifer were on to something—maybe we really did have a drinking problem. I felt more strongly than ever that enough was enough. But it was even more than a feeling—it was a conviction I think I had from reading the Bible and knowing it was not what I should be doing anymore.

When we talked about the number of times over the past two years Jake and Jennifer had suggested we stop drinking, we decided to give it a try. We didn't completely stop after the reunion, but we did decide that on August 31—the same date as our very first date—we'd stop for one month and see what happened. I needed to plan the date in advance so I could psyche myself up, the way you would plan for going on a diet or starting a new exercise routine. After all, I enjoyed drinking, but I was willing to go a month without it because I had been losing weight and feeling better since I'd cut back. But I also saw that Kathy had an issue with drinking, and I wanted to go through with it at least for her sake.

Leading up to our plan to stop drinking, Tim and I finished reading the Psalms and didn't want to stop, so we decided to start reading through the gospels. By then, I found myself more and more hungry to read the Bible. It was as though God had written things just for me, and I could feel myself changing on the inside. I was feeling more at peace and more certain than ever of God's love for me as being very real.

―――――――

As we went into September, we began our thirty-day commitment, and Kathy and I finally decided to give The Living Room a try. On our first visit, shortly after the service started, I said, "This isn't for me!" and left Kathy sitting by herself. When I walked toward the door to the foyer and opened it, there was a guy standing there and he asked, "What are you doing?" I said, "This isn't for me. They're singing weird songs and it's not what I'm used to." He said very calmly and matter-of-factly, "Oh, this *is* for you. Now go back and sit down. You need to be here." And I went back in and sat down. I couldn't believe I'd just let him tell me what to do, but I had.

After that day, we started attending on occasion—I still wasn't sure it was "the" church because of the worship songs. Hearing them didn't feel "churchy" enough for me compared to the traditional Lutheran churches we'd gone to over the years.

In the meantime, the end of our thirty days of not drinking was approaching, so of course the question came up: "Do we go another thirty days?" When we started the whole thing, my mindset was that we'd go back to drinking again, but we were doing so well. I suggested to Kathy that we do what I call the Ben Franklin Close—a process I used for years to close in the car business. What you do is, you take a blank piece of paper, draw a line down the middle, on one side write pros for buying the car, and on the other side write the cons. So that's what we did, and when we were finished, we had all pros for stopping drinking and no cons. We made the decision then to stop for another thirty days and see what happened.

By then, I still struggled with some anxiety, but it had improved a lot. I was even able to start working again. I also remember how good things were between Kathy and me. Up till then, we had searched and tried new things to help us change, but nothing stuck for very long. This time I think we knew our lives were finally changing for the better in a more lasting way. I had no idea, though, that what was about to come would change us forever.

It was the late fall of 2009, and Kathy I had continued to stop drinking—still thirty days at a time—and I continued to feel better. On a Sunday about that time we were at The Living Room when they started promoting an upcoming Christmas concert. They said the concert was about Christmas, only with a hook: to "win people to Christ." Interestingly, it was to be held at the same coliseum as a Kenny G concert we'd gone to two months before. I love Kenny G because I played saxophone in high school, but I remember my anxiety and claustrophobia were still bad, and I wasn't able to enjoy myself. The contrast between my life then and two months later was incredible.

The church leaders asked for volunteers to help put the show together and set up, but since it still wasn't really "my" church, I told them that Kathy and I would donate for the tickets and attend the concert to support them that way.

When the time came for the concert, we walked in, found our seats, and the performance began. Of course, there was music, and by the last song, called "The Lighthouse," I was captivated. The entire performance had touched my heart, but when they started singing that song, it was as though the lyrics shot straight into my soul:

> There's a lighthouse on the hillside
> That overlooks life's sea
> When I'm tossed, it sends out a light
> That I might see
> And the light that shines in darkness now
> Will safely lead us o'er
> If it wasn't for the lighthouse
> My ship would be no more

It seems that every one about us says,

Tear that old lighthouse down

The big ships just don't pass this way anymore

So there's no use in standin' round

Then my mind goes back to that one dark, stormy night

When just in time I saw the light

Yes, it was the light from that old lighthouse

That stands up there on the hill

And I thank God for the lighthouse

I owe my life to Him

Jesus is the lighthouse

And from the rocks of sin

He has shown a light around me

That I might clearly see

If it wasn't for the lighthouse

Tell me where would this ship be

I thank God for the lighthouse

I owe my life to Him

Jesus is the lighthouse

And from the rocks of sin

He has shown a light around me

That I might clearly see

If it wasn't for the lighthouse

Tell me where would this ship be[1]

---

1. "The Lighthouse," lyrics by Ronnie Hinson, © Songs Of Calvary Publishing, Dayspring Music, LLC.

As I listened, I could feel my heart begin to break. I was mesmerized and so moved. It was undeniable: the Holy Spirit came inside of me during that song. And when it was over, I reached down to Kath and said with tears in my eyes, "Babe, our lives are going to change forever. I felt the Holy Spirit come inside of me. We're going to go to this church, and we're going to serve Jesus!"

Since God had been working in my own heart leading up to that night, I knew deep down that Tim was right—things were really going to change. Our lives would never be the same.

———————

After years of going to church, after years of infidelities and drinking and drugs, after years of searching for something to help us fix our marriage (and fix Kathy!), we had *finally* reached the end of our search. Kathy and I both reached the point of finding the Lord. We just didn't know the difference between going to church and surrendering our lives to Christ and accepting Him as our personal Savior. We met Him heart-to-heart and soul-to-soul—me through music, and Kathy through reading the Word of God. The peace and hope we felt were indescribable.

Looking back, it seemed that no matter how bad or ugly our behavior, God continued to pursue us. We made baby steps throughout a years-long journey, yet as slow as we were, He didn't give up on us. He used different people to steer us toward Him, beginning with Pastor Gedde and continuing for years until Bob led us to read a chapter in Proverbs a day, and then shortly after to Bill, who led us to that Bible-teaching, Jesus-loving church. God didn't give up on us, and we knew things would be very different going forward.

And they were . . .

WHAT ABOUT YOU?

We think our story provides a clear message about the different levels of faith and belief we as Christians can have and how God works in them. For years, we thought that going to church was "it." Once the service was over, we'd go back to living the way we had been, and that was on our own terms. It's all we knew to do. In all that time, we didn't know that we could have a personal relationship with Jesus through His Holy Spirit being in us. He's not a faraway God; His presence is extremely close and personal down to the finest detail. "Jesus said, 'Peace be with you! As the Father has sent me, I am sending you.' And with that he breathed on them and said, 'Receive the Holy Spirit'" (John 20:21).

His Holy Spirit came into my broken heart through a song. It was a sudden aha moment that very quickly transformed me on the inside. For Kathy, her heart opened and transformed gradually through reading His Word. She even claimed her own life verse in 2 Corinthians 5:17, "If anyone is in Christ, the new creation has come: The old has gone, the new is here!" In reading His promises, she found Jesus, which shows there is no right or wrong way to accept Him as our Savior. What's important is that we simply accept Him in. Since I have, my life verse—one that Jake gave me—is Psalm 37:4, "Delight yourself in the LORD, and he will give you the desires of your heart" (ESV).

God's love is so big and never-ending, He is in constant pursuit of us. He wants everyone to know Him and to be in His tender care. Romans 8:38–39 says, "For I am convinced that neither death nor life, neither angels nor demons, neither the present nor the future, nor any powers, neither height nor depth, nor anything else in all creation, will be able to separate us from the love of God that is in Christ Jesus our Lord" (ESV). This verse rings true in our lives. No matter what we did that we're not proud of now, His love and forgiveness were there and waiting for us to receive. He has cleansed us—we are free from the guilt and shame we could be carrying. Instead, we live in freedom from those burdens, thanks to the truth expressed in John 3:17: "For God did not send his Son into the world to condemn the world, but to save the world through him." This is true for you too. He sees you and wants you to know the love He has for you. It is our hope that you can fully grasp this truth and claim it for yourself, no matter what you've done.

QUESTIONS FOR TRANSFORMATION————

- Given what we've just said, we ask, do you know Jesus personally? Have you accepted His Spirit into your own heart? If you haven't or you're not sure, all you must do is pray this simple prayer. Consider praying it with your spouse as a witness:

  > *Lord Jesus, I need You. I want to know You personally. Thank You for dying on the cross for my sins. I invite You into my life to be my Lord and Savior. Thank You for forgiving my sins and giving me eternal life. I surrender my life to You. Thank you, Jesus.*

- If you just prayed this prayer, welcome to the family! We are excited for you and the new life you will experience through knowing the Lord! Now it's time to go find a Jesus-loving, Bible-teaching church where you will be fed spiritually and have true fellowship with other believers.

- Also, will you reflect on your life and search your heart for anything you've done that you don't think God would forgive you for? Will you give it to Him now and be free from the guilt you've been carrying? Will you forgive yourself as well? Sometimes we can give our sin to God yet hang onto our own condemnation for it, but He wants us to be free from that.

- This was by far the biggest chapter in this book and in our lives. When you receive Jesus, you experience freedom you can only get from Him. Living a life of obedience to Him is a life of complete freedom. Do you want this kind of life? He is waiting!

PART TWO

16

The Transformation

*Don't copy the behavior and customs of this world, but
let God transform you into a new person by changing
the way you think. Then you will learn to know God's
will for you, which is good and pleasing and perfect.*

ROMANS 12:2 NLT

For the very first time in my life, I was anxiety free. I didn't
have to take drugs, I didn't need to drink, and I didn't
have to work out to try to feel normal. In fact, this was a new
feeling; it was a cleanness inside of me—this energy was
totally from within. I was always a positive person, but now
this positive energy felt almost out of control. I was excited
about life. I was excited about living. I was excited about Kath
and the things we were going to do, even though I had no clue
what they were yet. I thought about the "calling" we both
had on our lives and wondered even more what it was. Was it
simply going to The Living Room church and being involved
there? Or was it something else? I was searching again, but
this time it was to find out what *God* wanted for us. Life was

now a new mystery except for one thing: I knew things would be different because I was so different. My old self was gone.

This included how I would run our family business—I could sense it was not going to be the same, and I'd have to make many changes. This was a conviction for sure, even though at that time convictions were very new to me.

In Case You Were Wondering . . .
KATHY

Transformation is just that, transforming. I had no clue what making Jesus the Lord of my life entailed. This was just the beginning, and I would soon find out that the more I learned and grew in Christ, the more I would need to learn. You see, God doesn't transform us all at once. I had no idea the journey He would take Tim and me on continuing up to today. I had no idea how hard, yet fulfilling, things would be being a believer. The beauty of it was, Tim and I had found Jesus, and He was smack dab in the center of our marriage for the first time! I finally knew the love of Christ and therefore knew how to love Tim.

At this point, TJ and Blake were minority partners at the dealership—TJ as Sales Manager and Blake as soon-to-be New Car Manager. Yes, they were my sons, but they both held high positions in the day-to-day operations, which I respected. However, I was still the owner and still their dad, and the new changes of serving the Lord brought a whole new set of challenges and dynamics I didn't see coming. In fact, my excitement wasn't that welcome. My new ways were so different from the way the boys were taught, so I really couldn't blame the initial pushback, but at this point the changes were not a choice for me.

My first change was to be closed on Sundays from that point on—not a usual thing in the car business! After all, weekends can be the highest-selling days since people are off work, and I eliminated one of them. We still managed to meet our quotas, but even so, my sons initially didn't like this, but eventually they came on board. (Later, the BMW manufacturer was not happy.)

Another thing I did was, there were at least a half dozen TVs all around the building that ran ESPN sports all the time, and I wanted that changed, so I delegated someone to create a program with a track of scriptures that would circulate verses on the screens instead of sports.

But then there was the issue of the radio dial . . .

Normally we had country or jazz playing across the floor, but I went back into our electronic room and changed it to The Message, a Christian station. Soon I noticed that when I came into the office in the mornings, I'd find that someone had changed it back to a secular station. Frustrated, I'd quickly change it back. While this went on for a while, Kath got a call from TJ.

Yeah, TJ called and said, "Mom, you gotta stop Dad!"

"Wait, what are you talking about, TJ?"

"Mom, we're trying to sell cars here, and Dad is talking to everyone about Jesus. And he's praying with the customers! This is a BMW dealership, Mom." Then he said, "I'm pretty sure Jesus even had 'normal' conversations with people . . ."

I said with a smile, "Well, TJ, that's your dad, and I can't tell him to stop doing that!"

In just a few short months, pushback came from TJ and Blake as well as from other management pressuring me that people were going to quit because of all the changes, but this didn't cause me to back down. I was nice about it but said if anyone wanted to quit, I would write them a letter of recommendation. In the meantime, the issue with the radio station continued until finally one day I got fed up, went into the tech room, and left a note on the dial: "You have a camera looking down on you, and whoever changes this radio station doesn't work here anymore." I signed "Tim Bush" at the bottom.

A little later I heard Blake over the intercom say, "Tim Bush to the sales office." I walked in, he asked me to sit, and then he closed the door and said, "Dad, I don't even know who you are anymore. Everything you do is totally different, and I don't understand how to communicate with you."

I listened to him vent and when he finished, I said very calmly, "Son, do you like me better now, or did you like me better before, the way I used to be?"

"*Well*, when you say it *that* way . . . I like you better now . . ."

"Okay, enough said. Let's go back to work and *leave the radio alone!*" And he did leave it alone. But he didn't know I was about to take the radio to another level.

Thoughts from the Kids . . .
BLAKE

Who was this guy, and what did He do with my dad? Up until now, I had always relied on my dad at the dealership to help us with tough customers and to help make the car deals happen! At this point I didn't even know if he was trying to sell cars anymore or convert customers to Christianity. I had enough and when I called him in the sales office, I was going to fix him. After the question was asked about liking him before or now, I had a huge epiphany that I wouldn't ever want my dad to go back to the way he was before, and whatever he had turned into was special. I just didn't know what that meant yet.

Next to the sales office was the service center where all the service technicians worked. They each had their own stall and played their own radios. One day while walking through, I heard songs with cuss words and other foul language—nothing that was appropriate. I talked to the service manager and said, "Look, this doesn't work for me anymore, and I need you to tell the guys to change their stations." He said, "Tim, if I do that, they're going to quit!"

I said, "I'm really sorry that has to happen. That's not my intent and I'm glad to give anyone who quits a letter of recommendation. I just want us all on the same page. In fact, I'm going to put really nice speakers in the shop so the *whole* dealership system can be on The Message station. So you may as well tell all your guys to take their stereos home. This is nonnegotiable."

It wasn't long before I had the new system installed, tuned to the Christian station, and playing over the entire dealership, including outside. Not one person quit. In fact, one Monday when I got to the office, the service manager came to me and said a technician wanted to talk to me. When I walked into his stall, he said, "Tim, you're not going to believe this. I went to a conference over the weekend called A Walk with Christ, and I gave my life to Jesus. And I want you to know I'm really thankful I get to work in this environment!"

You just never know when you plant seeds where they're going to fall and how God's going to water them.

In Case You Were Wondering ...
TIM

It was like waking up and being a completely different person, and the old guy was not only gone, but he was also transformed to tell others of how he felt. That was me in a nutshell. Instead of searching for my happiness, it was now about my calling and finding the Lord's path for our lives and sharing with others about what happened to me, and how it was available to all. My obedience to the Lord was now growing through so many life changes that you normally wouldn't think possible just weeks prior. Kath and I were all in.

———

While Tim was making radical changes at the dealership, life for me took a big turn as well. First, Tim and I and most of the kids and grandkids started going to church regularly. In fact, Tim and I went to all three Sunday services. I also changed the music and shared what God was doing in my life at my spa. I lost a few clients, but most of them stayed, and I gained new ones. When I wasn't working, I stayed home and watched TV—all the sermons and Christian talk shows I could take in—a big change from the soap operas I used to watch! I was so excited, I even started looking into going to seminary. I knew I had so much to learn and didn't want to waste any more time. When Tim got home at the end of each day, I would share all that I had learned. I felt so alive—nothing like I had ever experienced before.

I also had a new experience with God convicting me of something that was very personal: removing my breast implants. I had had the implants for ten or so years, and it was approaching the time to have them replaced. I'd already made the appointment a few weeks before our conversion at Christmas, but as it got closer to the surgery in January, I began to feel unsettled. At the same time, I felt hesitant to dive into women's groups at church because I didn't want any of them to know this about me—I was afraid I'd be judged. So I kept my distance at first as I began to wonder if I was doing the right thing by replacing the implants. I know now it was God convicting me about having them removed, and I should've listened.

I went ahead with the surgery to replace them, and as soon as I got home, I knew I'd done the wrong thing. Please let me be clear: replacing the implants was wrong for me because it's not what God wanted me to do. It was the same way I felt after drinking all night at Tim's thirty-year reunion. I knew deep down He wanted me to stop, and now He wanted me not to keep my implants, but I kept them anyway.

After I had the surgery and began to heal, I eventually got involved at church and joined a women's Bible study. Years before I couldn't bring myself to do Bible studies because I felt so intimidated, but it didn't take long for me not only to look forward to attending but to jump right into a Beth Moore study on Revelation!

Over time, I finally told Tim about my conviction about my implants, and as supportive as he was, I still waited another few years before I finally had them removed once and for all. And at that moment, I knew I had done the right thing. My identity was wrapped up in what I looked like, and God was teaching me something different—that my identity was who I was in Him. Since then I've learned to recognize what a conviction feels like. I've also become much more sensitive and willing to trust that God has my best interests at heart and not to turn away from His leading. Following a conviction from God is always the right reason to do something, even when it doesn't make sense or I don't agree.

———

By February and after spending a lot of time at church, I was approached by Pastor Mel, who held a small group at his home called Financial Advisory Team (FAT), and he wanted to know if I'd join. Up to that time, the church had been meeting in a casino connected to a bowling alley, and this group met to raise funds and find a new facility we could grow into. So I started to serve in the group, once a week to start. Then I became so convicted about really applying myself, I started spending up to twenty hours a week working with them in addition to running the dealership and other business entities.

A little later that spring while the FAT team worked on raising funds, the church had an amazing seven-week sermon series on the fruit of the Spirit that *really* touched my heart. When it was over, I thought of a young woman who worked in the dealership office; she was from Ukraine. Her name was Liliya, she was a believer, and I knew she was a gifted artist.

After hearing the sermon series, I approached her and asked, "Liliya, have you heard of the fruit of the Spirit?" Without missing a beat, she said, "Do you mean Galatians 5:22–23?" She knew exactly where it was in the Bible!

I said, "Liliya, would you consider doing a painting for each of the fruit to hang here at the dealership? I want to take down all the pictures of cars and put your paintings in their place." She said she would think about it.

A couple of days later, our office manager and our daughter-in-law Amanda came to me and said Liliya wanted to talk to me about some paintings. I went to her thinking that, if she agreed, she'd want to talk about how much it would cost me. To my surprise, when I saw her, she said, "I want you to know I want to do the paintings, but it's probably going to take me a long time because, first, I need to pray about what I'm going to paint. After praying I need to wait for God to give me a dream, and then I'll paint my dream. That's how I have to do it." Needless to say, there was no ask about the cost, and I said, "That's great. Let's do it, and you take as long as you need."

A few months later, Liliya arrived at work and said, "Good morning, Tim. The paintings are done, and they're in the back of my car." I walked out to her car with her, helped take them out, and saw that they were nothing short of amazing. I hung them in the dealership right away.

I wasn't worried about the cost, but when I asked her what I owed her, she said, "Oh, no, I could never be paid for these. If you want to just cover my expenses of $250, that would be good."

On a side note, thinking about the paintings, talking about this story, when Kath and I look at all the "things" we have, those paintings are priceless to us. They will always stay in our family because they were part of our transformation.

Well, with all of the changes I made in the dealership, even with the initial pushback received, not a week went by that I didn't get called to the front counter to meet a customer who would say, "I want you to know, I love the music, I love what's going on here, I love the feeling I get when I walk in." Without hesitation, I can say 100 percent of the feedback received from customers was positive. Not one negative. That said, we got plenty of negative comments from the BMW manufacturer . . .

WHAT ABOUT YOU?

Whether salvation comes in stages because of a history of church or religion, as Kath's did, or more quickly, like mine did, sooner or later His Spirit will change your heart. Even if you've lived a "clean" life for the most part, He wants us to be our very best, and He will work in us to do what most of us resist: change! Not only is it challenging for the one who is changing, but also for the people who are directly affected by it, as was the case for our family, employees, and extended family. There can be pushback, so at some point we may come face-to-face with our willingness to trust God in those times.

For me, God wanted me to change in a deeply personal way—in a way that didn't directly affect anyone but myself. But it was still hard. Before knowing the Lord, I put my identity in my looks and abilities. But what He wanted to make clear was that my true and unyielding identity is in Him. I had to learn I was "fearfully and wonderfully made" just the way He made me, and that goes against what society tells us on a daily basis. I'm glad I embraced the change He convicted me to make, but what about you? Have you been able to trust Him enough to do the same in your life?

QUESTIONS FOR TRANSFORMATION————

- Assuming you've accepted Christ and the Holy Spirit into your heart, can you think of ways He has transformed your thinking, your perspective, and the way you live now from before? How have those changes benefited you? In what ways has it been hard?

- Philippians 1:6 says, "He who began a good work in you will carry it on to completion until the day of Christ Jesus." That means our transformation doesn't end until we pass from this earth. On that note, can you think of any ways He is convicting you now to change a habit or thought pattern? Are you resistant to change, or are you willing to trust what He's doing in you?

- What are you willing to give up personally or as a married couple? How can you encourage each other as you do so?

17

The Cost

"[Families] will be divided, father against son and son against father, mother against daughter and daughter against mother, mother-in-law against daughter-in-law and daughter-in-law against mother-in-law."

LUKE 12:53

Looking back on our lives before Christ, we made slow baby steps forward and many steps backward over a period of decades before finally meeting and committing our lives to Him. But once that happened, it's as though we had to wear seat belts— He sped our pace and didn't waste any time aligning us "just so," so we'd know without a doubt how and where He wanted to use us. As we continued to grow, we had some twists and turns to maneuver to finally know our calling. In the meantime, we learned that not everyone was in support of our new journey. This new faith in our lives looked familiar—like just another new thing we were trying. Family members wondered how long it would last this time, and rightfully so. It was our pattern—always trying

something new. Even so, we kept moving forward in our relation-
ship with Christ and the adventure He had in store.

In Case You Were Wondering ...
TIM

Mel had told me to consider praying with Kath, and not just at meals. He encouraged me and said it was something I could do, that basically the Lord would load my lips. I read a book on prayer and started praying more immediately. In the car business it takes ninety days to make a habit, but this was different. This was an instant habit. It became a lifetime non-negotiable step of obedience to the Lord. Never a day goes by that Kath and I don't pray together. This and reading God's Word has been instrumental in the growth of our Christ-centered marriage.

While Tim was busy serving on the FAT team and I con-
tinued to soak in all the Bible study I could, we also began to
pray together every day—or at least Tim led us in prayer while
I prayed silently. It was also a time we were excited to hear our
pastor announce a baptism that would take place that summer.
We both knew this was our next step: to get baptized and show
everyone that we had made Jesus our Lord and Savior. We were
so excited because it was going to be done in the Columbia River—
where Tim's brother Ned had been baptized two years before. We
thought of how special that would be. The thought made it even
more special and sentimental, especially for Tim. So that's what
we did. On August 25, 2010, we got baptized in the river together. I
was so nervous because I knew I had to tell everyone why I wanted

to get baptized, plus I knew there were going to be a lot of people watching, but I trusted that the Holy Spirit would help. It was an amazing day and hard at the same time. Some family members we'd invited didn't come because it wasn't something they believed in, and my feelings were hurt. And as we continued to grow, resistance from our family kept growing as well.

Tim and I did what we could to lead our family to embrace Jesus and His Holy Spirit, and our kids and grandkids were receptive, but other family members kept questioning what kind of church it was we were going to. It was so different from the religious rituals they were familiar with. Things finally came to a head one day on the phone with one of my family members when the conversation turned to yelling at me, expressing their dislike of the conservative stance our church took on a particular social issue. The negativism and pressure I'd been getting took a toll on my nerves, and I broke down in tears and hung up.

In Case You Were Wondering . . .
KATHY

As hard as all the family difficulties were and some continue to be, God continues to be faithful to me. I realize the importance of staying in relationship with Jesus and reading God's Word is so important. Sometimes praying for these relationships is the best I can do. I know that God is ultimately in control, not me. Having sisters and brothers in Christ keeps me encouraged. I used to try and push through bad relationships on my own. I have learned, as I have grown in Christ, to wait on Him, and that's where my peace comes from.

The beauty that came from all the family difficulties was that our church became our family, and I pressed in even more. By this time, I wanted a break from all the stress and friction I'd been going through, so when the pastor gave a final announcement about a mission trip to Rwanda a group had been planning, I thought it'd do me good to break away from everyone for a while. It turned out there was one seat left on the plane. So I took it.

This was a very big step for me—I didn't know a single person that was going, except for Pastor Mel, and Tim wouldn't be there with me. But off I went and for the next seventeen days, God continued to work in my heart in ways I never imagined.

Our missions group made such special relationships with the people there. We shared the gospel with them, we helped in the building of a house, and we did daily devotions together. The pastor even asked me to lead a devotion! Speaking in front of people without Tim beside me was a giant step outside my comfort zone, but I did it. It was all so spiritual—I felt the presence of God on a whole new level, and my relationship with God deepened all the more. The relationships with the team members were incredible too.

I was so changed by the experience; I wondered if God was calling me to mission work. Seeing the poor and how little they had, yet their faith and relationship with Christ was so strong . . . I left wanting more of what they had spiritually.

After arriving home, I was soaking in a hot bath when I started to cry. I told Tim I wanted to sell my wedding ring and help the poor in Africa. Of course, Tim said we could support them, and I didn't have to sell my ring. That trip helped me put the bigger picture of my faith and family struggles into perspective. The issues I had with them were still there, but I was able to view the problems differently and start trusting that God was, and is, in control.

_____

While Kath was on her mission trip, I stayed busy at the dealership and worked with the FAT team to raise funds for a new church building. We did whatever we could to make money—in a God-honoring way—and it's a good thing we were building momentum because the casino we had been leasing gave us notice, and we had only a short time to move out. This was the kind of thing that made me thrive—I even thought it was, or at least was part of, my calling. So we moved into a temporary location in Richland while we worked hard to raise funds to buy a place where we could grow.

At the same time, summer was approaching, and my friend Steve came to me about a marriage ministry class his church was doing called iMarriage by Andy Stanley. He said, "Tim, you guys ought to think about doing this curriculum at your church. It's been effective for us."

I talked to Kath about it, then went to Mel and Monte and told them I thought it was something we were supposed to do—it really made sense to me. It so happens that leadership was working on a new summer series of classes and thought the timing couldn't have been better, so they added iMarriage as an option, not really knowing what to expect.

When Tim told me about iMarriage, he was pretty excited and even said he wondered if marriage ministry was where our calling was. I looked at him and said, "Well, you can do it by yourself!" Of course, Tim couldn't do it by himself, but it shows you how closed off I was to the idea. He said the pastors wanted us to do it, plus he thought it would be good to share our story at the same time we led the study. I said, "Well, as far as sharing our story, you can do the talking, and I'll support you."

We soon launched the series, and the very first night there were thirty-six couples in attendance! As planned, Tim did all the talking, and when the night ended and we were driving home, we talked about how well it had gone. I told Tim what I thought he should have said and what he should say at the next session, but then I stopped myself. I suddenly felt the Holy Spirit and heard Him say, "You know, Kathy, you can talk." After letting those words soak in, I looked at Tim and said, "You know what, Babe? I'll be part of this and do some of the talking." (Tim says I haven't stopped talking since!)

Well, we went on to complete the series with close to 100 percent attendance, which is almost unheard of for a summer series. The series itself was excellent and was very effective, even for us. By the time we finished, we had a feeling it was only the beginning of what God had in store for us in marriage ministry. But even though we had taken our first step into our calling, we still didn't quite know it yet.

In the meantime, Tim remained busy with FAT and fundraising for our new church building.

The FAT team and I had to get as creative as we could to keep raising funds and using the dealership to help—and the Lord *really* blessed us.

First, we closed the dealership on a Friday afternoon, then I closed the service department on Saturday, and held a concert Saturday night. Then we had church and Sunday school the next morning inside the dealership. That one event alone raised $110,000! (And no, I didn't get permission from the BMW manufacturer!) In a short time, we raised just under half a million dollars in five months, which is amazing for a 350-member church. By fall, all of our labor paid off: we'd raised enough down payment money to buy Old Bethlehem Lutheran School, which was built in 1955 and perfect for renovation for our needs.

Once we bought the property, never will I forget our church body circling and praying over it. It felt like God was preparing us to do big things in serving Him. We were all in, every one of us. Plus, the camaraderie of those who served on FAT was amazing. We had been through so much together while trying to raise money. It was like a small group of people banded together on mission for Jesus.

――――――――

Even with all the work related to the new church facility, we continued to press forward with new ministries for growth. Mel and Monte said they wanted the church to start doing small groups, but they didn't know much about how to start and manage them. So we reached out to Real Life Church in North Idaho because we heard that they knew all about doing them to a high level.

Soon the other guys on the team and I drove out to meet with them, and it turned out to be the right thing to do. The people there were willing to teach us and share their material, as well as share some of their success stories. When we got back, Kath and I and four other couples started the first small groups. We launched with a study called Starting Point by Andy Stanley. As all of this began, Monte and I took a couple trips to other churches to fine-tune what the Lord had for us. It was exciting. We dreamed big!

Starting small groups was exactly what Kath and I needed, and we raised the thought that maybe *that* was our calling. We weren't sure, but we did know that the friends we made in that environment were some of the first solid Christian friends we'd made. We still connect with some of them today—all because of what God started back in 2011. Most of our drinking friends were gone, and we were excited to have new ones who shared our love for Jesus. Plus Kath and I made friends together. We finally knew what it felt like to experience fellowship with other believers—something we hadn't known about before.

It was also about this time in our spiritual growth when one night I was about to pray for Kath and me—I'd been praying for us for ten months by then—and Kath said, "Hey, before you start to pray, can I ask you a question?"

"Sure," I said.

"Could you leave a little spot at the end, before you say, 'In Jesus' name', so I can pray?"

"Sure!"

And she's never stopped praying.

———————

On a side note, it was through our small group we ended up getting our sweet dog. Kath and I had been arguing about getting a dog—I wanted one, and she didn't. All our married years before, Kath had bad experiences with our dogs, and I was never any help with them. We had been going through the Starting Point study when one evening we were discussing the grace of God, and for some reason the topic of me wanting a dog came up, and the group kept saying, "Come on, Kathy, let Tim have a dog." A few days later Kath said, "Don't hold me to this, but I'm kind of thinking I want a dog." (Kath would say the reason she decided to get a dog is because our small group was praying for her to change her mind, and it worked!) I said, "Really? What kind?" She said, "I'm thinking of a Labradoodle because they don't shed, they're hypoallergenic, and they don't get very big."

I wanted a lab, but of course, the *last* thing I wanted was a dog that had the word *doodle* on the end of it! But I was at least willing to talk about it. Kath had the owner of one bring the puppy and its mother to our house so we could meet. And when she sat that little puppy in my lap, I fell in love with her immediately. We named her Amazing Grace, and we still have her today.

————————

As we continued to pursue God and how He wanted to use us, our fire for Him grew even more. A friend gave me a copy of Experiencing God *by Henry Blackaby, and as I read it, I wondered,* Why didn't anyone tell me any of this about God before?! *It was so life-changing for me that Tim read it, and then our small group went through the Bible study together. Tim and I were basically full throttle between learning all we could about God, developing new relationships with other believers, serving on FAT, and attending church whenever we could. But while our joy increased, by Easter of 2011, more problems about our zeal for God began to surface— this time with our kids. In spite of the stress it brought, we at least had one blessing to look forward to: Tim's fiftieth birthday. Not only was he alive and growing in Christ (given all he'd been through before he got saved), but I planned a surprise he didn't anticipate: the renewal of our wedding vows. We were in Mexico celebrating when I flew in our pastor to perform the ceremony, along with his wife and their son, who did the music. I brought in all the kids and grandkids, and Tim's longtime friend from Boise showed up to surprise him too. When all the surprise guests arrived, Tim was very*

confused until I looked at him and asked if he'd marry me again.
He lit up and said "Yes!" It was a beautiful ceremony—more than
I could have ever dreamed of. On top of that, this was something I
had planned without Tim's help, which was a big deal for me. God
was stretching and growing me in new ways.

After twenty-nine years of being married, we gathered and
renewed our vows, only this time, instead of depending on all the
vices we'd tried before to hold us together, we put Christ at the center.

Sadly, shortly after we got home from our trip, problems con-
tinued with our kids—we were way too "churchy" in their eyes.
They were increasingly uncomfortable with our new faith. But ...
what were we supposed to do? We weren't going to lighten up—we
had never been better or happier. Even so, doors that used to be
open to us were shut, and we weren't able to see our kids or four
grandkids for a year and a half. It was a harsh reality to face, and
it hit home very hard about the cost involved when you go all in for
Christ. I think of the question, "Whom will I serve today, God or
man?" And as convicted as I was (and still am) that the answer is
God, it was a very difficult time of separation. It caused us to be so
thankful for our church family, and I held to the truth that even
Jesus had difficult times with his family. Why should I presume it
wouldn't happen to us?

Thoughts from the Kids ...
JIMMY

Tricia and I were the kids that didn't have a relationship
with Mom and Dad for over a year. When they became
on fire for the Lord, we went through a period where
we felt extremely judged. While we were not involved

Tim being
baptized

Kathy being
baptized

After our
baptisms

Ned's plaque on the car wash in his memory

Tim, Kathy, Kate, and Mady at the car wash dedication in honor of Ned

Our first small group

Praying over the property for The Living Room Church

Fundraiser
at The Living
Room Church

Fundraiser at the BMW dealership for the church

Vow renewal of friends

Our vow
renewal in
Mexico

Kathy's mission trip to Rwanda

Our trip to
Rwanda

The two of us
on a mission
trip

Fruit of the Spirit paintings

Our first marriage event, in Big Fork, Montana

A marriage class we held at Bethel

Mel and Denise's marriage renewal in Deer Lake

Weekend to Remember

Rock Your Marriage event

Vertical Marriage with Dave and Ann

Blake and Cara's wedding at the Lake Place

2017 Marriage Ministry Christmas party

Art of
Marriage
class

Art of Marriage event at The War Room

Stepping Up at The War Room

Marriage Ministry at The War Room

Art of Marriage event in Villa Park

Christmas event at the War Room with Justin and Falon

Tim hunting with Dennis in South Dakota

Tim hunting with Dennis and David in South Dakota

Kathy, Shell, and our writer Lisa

Kathy at a women's retreat with the FamilyLife ladies

Marriage event in Arizona

Marriage event in North Carolina

The family together after the send-off at our church

Our family

Christians as they were, we had been doing our best and taking our kids to church for years. Like most dads, I was struggling to provide a balance between providing for my family and being present with my family. I made it a priority to be home every night by 5 p.m. Suddenly, everything I did felt not good enough. It got to the point where I told Tricia that I couldn't handle it anymore, and I didn't want their unsolicited advice. I couldn't believe that parents who were mostly absent during their own kids' upbringing were going to tell us how to be good Christian parents. Also, at this time we still weren't sure if this new change was going to last. This led to us setting boundaries with Mom and Dad and resulted in our family not having a relationship for over a year. Thankfully, we were eventually able to heal, and I believe our relationships are stronger now than they were before.

WHAT ABOUT YOU?

Everyone who comes to faith in Christ faces a change in family dynamics, especially when they don't understand and share your new beliefs. That was certainly the case for us, and it was a difficult test we had to work through. I think of how right after Jesus was baptized, he went into the wilderness for forty days of temptation. In a similar way, we will be challenged early on because when we have the Holy Spirit in us, we're convicted of doing away with our old selves and lifestyles to make room for how God wants us to live and serve. Change always brings challenge.

Can you relate? We imagine your head is nodding if you have your own difficult story to tell. But it is good to know you're not alone. It is often part of the Christian journey. Not only does Christ understand, but He is faithful to honor our steadfast commitment to Him. God never tells us this Christian life will be easy. He says it will be hard, but that He will give us peace, His peace, to sustain us every step of the way.

QUESTIONS FOR TRANSFORMATION————

- Looking back, what struggle did you face within your family when you became a Christian? Some of you may be in one now and could use some encouragement. Will you talk about what pain it has caused and pray together for healing? Have you reached out to other believers for support and prayer?

- To take things a step further, are you making it a priority to pray for those family members? That is what we did and are still doing, and our relationship with our kids and grandkids has been healed. Thank You, Jesus.

- Have you been convicted of or even asked straight out to serve in a new way in church or in your community that seems overwhelming? Maybe you don't feel qualified because you've never done it before? Take time now to talk about your fears or concerns and commit any new opportunities you have to prayer.

18

The Calling

You are a chosen people, a royal priesthood, a holy nation,
God's special possession, that you may declare the praises of
him who called you out of darkness into his wonderful light.

1 PETER 2:9

The FAT team and I had sleeves rolled up and were excited to get started on the renovation of the Lutheran school the church had purchased. We'd raised a lot of money for the down payment, but there was a lot to do to convert rooms and make other updates, plus there were code require- ments and lots of architectural design changes to fit our needs, so we had to allot funds carefully to stay within budget. I brought my architect and friend to do the architectural stuff, which he did at a very reduced cost. Then we also had to get a loan, which was complicated, but that was my forte. It took going to *seven* banks before finally getting one to take us on. Our team worked tirelessly not to miss any details, and we kept each other accountable to our tasks; many of us had different levels of experience and gifts. We had become close-knit, and we counted on each other.

That's why I was taken aback when, while out of town, I found out some additional changes were planned without me knowing. I soon realized that only scratched the surface of some difficult circumstances I didn't see coming, and my immaturity as a Christian came out for sure. As disharmony grew, I also felt a tug from God to step down and prepare for another role He had in store. I've learned since then that sometimes that's what it takes to get us to move from serving in one role into another, and that was the case with me. Quitting was, and is, not in my DNA, but I felt like this change was from the Lord, which made it different. That said, there was some hurt I had to work through. While I did, my mind didn't shut down—I got a vision to start my own church. I mentioned it to Kath, but she stayed quiet and didn't jump in with enthusiasm. Even so, I knew she was praying for me.

As time passed, I got super charged with passion— nothing was going to stop me. I got even more fired up about building and operating my own church, especially because I was going to do things *my* way. I would build it on the property next to my dealership; I would have amazing music; I would bring in different speakers to lead the services. I, I, I, I, I. And I knew I could do it. It was just another business venture, right? Wrong!

I was so self-absorbed with being right and doing things my way, and pretty sure now that the Lord was very disappointed in this new believer who hadn't even read the complete Bible yet. I was used to being a winger—or an improvisor—and I didn't want any help that could take me off track. I knew all the work was on my shoulders, and I honestly didn't care what anyone thought, even Kath, which was totally wrong not to be in sync with her.

At this point in our journey, we were reading the Bible every day, but one thing that concerned me was that Tim wasn't studying the Bible. I was engulfed in Christian TV and podcasts, studying, and learning more every day. What had happened at the church was so hurtful to us both, but especially to Tim. What I saw was that Tim's leadership was over-the-top and many people were intimated by that. But as Tim talked about starting a church on his own, my first thought was, You haven't even read the Bible through completely, and you want to start a church? *So, yes, I stayed quiet and prayed. I knew and trusted God would work it out. I also knew that the hurt we felt would not keep us away from church as it had in past years.*

One day I was having lunch in a Mexican restaurant in a building I owned, and a friend, Bob Nash, who saw me walked over and introduced me to his friend Pastor Dave. I had heard from Bob many times over the years that Dave was a really good Bible teacher at a church called Bethel. It was the largest church in Richland and maybe even in Tri-Cities. Bethel had held the funeral service for our nephew a few years before. I also remembered that Ned went to Bible study with some men there. I remembered seeing Dave in action that Easter years before when they had a bridge to walk across, which Kath talked about earlier, so it was nice to get to meet him. After the introduction, I finished my lunch and went back to the dealership, not thinking anything of it.

Not long after getting back to the office, my phone rang, and I picked up.

"Hey, Tim, this is Dave Bechtel—Bob just introduced us. I'm sixty years old and thinking about buying a BMW convertible, and I'd like to talk to you about it."

"Okay," I said. "Come on over."

He came to my office and we talked a while about BMWs and some details he wanted, then at one point he stopped and said, "You know, I can sense in my spirit that there's something going on you might like to talk to me about." I said, "No . . . I don't want to talk to you about anything." Given what I'd just been through at church, I then said, "Besides, the last thing I want to do is be friends with another pastor."

"Well, Tim, we don't have to be friends, but I am a pastor, and you can talk to me about anything. It'll just stay between you and me."

I said, "Look Dave, you don't get it. I'm going to start my own church, right here on my property. I won't have any debt. I'll have the most amazing music. I'm going to pay pastors to come in and speak. I'm going to build it and run it exactly the *way* I want it and *how* I want it."

He said, "Well, I'd like to help you."

"No, Dave, you didn't hear me. I'm going to build it right here in Richland." When I said that, I thought he'd get the hint that it'd compete with his church and that he'd back off. But he said, "You know, I want you to know, first, this is God's church, right?"

"Of *course*, it is."

"Well, I keep hearing you say 'I' this and 'I' that, and I want you to know that if this church were right next door to

Bethel—the church that I'm part of—I would still want to help you. Even better than that, there is a group of five of us men who meet at church at six o'clock in the morning, and I think those guys would want to help you too. Is six too early for you?

"No, I get up at 4:30!"

"Well, we read the One-Year Bible together. Do you have one?"

"No, but I can get one."

"If you come and meet the guys, I'm sure they'll want to help you with this church."

So I bought a copy of the One-Year Bible and went the following Tuesday. I didn't know it then, but walking into that hospitality room and meeting those men would build some of the most amazing connections of my life. They are still my brothers and among my closest friends now, since that first meeting in February 2012.

A few weeks later, Kath and I decided to go to church at Bethel, and she made it clear right away it was the church we needed to go to. She liked Dave's leadership and felt he would appreciate my leadership skills without feeling intimidated by them, which I needed. At the same time, I saw how God was working in those men on Tuesday mornings, and my need to start a new church—*my* church—faded. I could see that God was already working at Bethel and in the Tuesday men's group. It was my crisis of belief to be in that church and get back to finding out what my calling was, as I was still searching. It wasn't what I'd been doing the previous two years, so what was it?

In Case You Were Wondering . . .
KATHY

I remember this time like it was yesterday. My hunger for Christ was incredible. I couldn't get enough. I remember asking a friend if it was okay that I felt Jesus was like a drug. I wanted more and more of Him. I also remember thinking I knew more about God than Tim did, like I was doing a better job because I was studying more. As God continues to grow me, I know that I am no better than anyone. That is pure pride. So, when Tim started talking about starting his own church, I really had to keep my mouth shut and pray that God would work in Tim. And sure enough, He did. God moved us to an incredible church where we were fed meat. This church is where God moved in me and made it clear that Tim and I would do marriage ministry and share our story for the glory of God.

————

Not long after we started going to Bethel, I felt a tug that we needed to be doing marriage ministry the way we had at The Living Room. At the same time we had an amazing surprise by Easter: our baby Blake, who was a grown and married man, gave his life to the Lord at an altar call that day! That meant all our kids were saved, and we were so excited. Praise Jesus!

By middle of 2013, fifteen months after joining the men's group, I mentioned marriage ministry to Dave, and he asked, "What do you want to do about it, Tim?" It wasn't that simple because he knew about Kath's and my past before we got saved, so there could be pushback from some people. What was great, though, is that Dave said he was prepared to take any hits on our behalf. He said, "If you think you really want to go down this road, there's a leadership conference called Catalyst in mid-October, and we'll set you and Kathy up to go." And I said, "Yes!" I already knew I wanted to use the iMarriage material—it was so successful before—so the thought of learning more about improving my leadership skills was exciting. Even Andy Stanley himself—the author of iMarriage—was scheduled to speak. *Stoked* would be an understatement.

I wondered, after moving to a new church, would Tim still want to dive into marriage ministry? Sure enough, once again, he started talking that way. This time, though, we were in the largest church in our town, so that meant a lot of people to be in front of. My sense was that Tim and I would need to get better equipped. I googled "Christian marriage conferences" and found one called A Weekend to Remember held by FamilyLife, so I signed us up. Also on their website was a bonus: the Love Like You Mean It Cruise. It was sailing in February, and there was going to be over one hundred hours of marriage teaching and entertainment. I was so excited about going and soaking in all that information.

The Weekend to Remember conference was in Coeur d'Alene, Idaho, in November, and Kath and I were both excited to attend. We invited two other couples, Dave and Linda and Bob and Jeannie, from Bethel who also wanted to do marriage ministry with us. As I said before, I'd already decided to use iMarriage material, so I was determined to go with the mindset of not learning a bunch of new things, but learning *one* new thing we could add to what we were already going to do.

When we got there and were eating dinner the first night, I said to everyone, "Okay, guys, we need to spend this time with our wives and learn one thing we can take from this time that will help other marriages. Let's all take notes and talk later about what it will be." And I confess, Kath and I both thought our marriage was so good and solid, it would be interesting to learn that one new thing. But we discovered from the material they used that there was a lot we needed to work on for ourselves—more than just one thing. Their material made an incredible, profound, totally unexpected impact we couldn't ignore. We were almost overwhelmed!

When the conference started, I remember sitting in my chair and the thought hit me: it was the first time we'd gone to anything for our marriage when we weren't a mess. It was the first time we were in the mindset of receiving rich and valuable information from God, not some counselor. It felt so peaceful that we were in such a good place. In fact, it was a time I really felt God move in me so powerfully, I began to see clearly and believed that Tim and I were being called to marriage ministry. Before that, It felt like I was being dragged into these settings by Tim, but at that moment, it was God making it clear that this was what He wanted us to do. He said, "You're going to do this with Tim."

As the conference ended, they provided a lot of additional resources to take home and use, so we ended up purchasing bags of books, including one called *Stepping Up* by Dennis Rainey (more on this book later as it was a life-changer for me and many others). I remember calling Pastor Dave around six o'clock Sunday morning and saying, "Dave, I think this is from the Lord: We can't do iMarriage. I think we need to be doing The Art of Marriage by FamilyLife. Just the few clips we've seen and looking at the manual has made such an impact on Kath and me. What do you think?"

He said, "Tim, if you think this is from the Lord, then I think it's from the Lord. Let's do it." It meant a lot to me to hear him say that without question. The impact that man had on my life, his support of our thoughts and ideas, was huge to me. As Kath and I drove home—in silence almost all the way—our calling was becoming clear. It was one of the first times in my life when I felt so filled with the Holy spirit, I literally had no words coming out of my mouth. Kath's either. We were both completely spent because we both knew what was on the horizon.

———

As soon as we returned, we started promoting a six-week marriage series that would begin in January, and Kath and I literally argued over how big it should be. I wanted it to be three hundred people—a huge *splash* in the biggest event room there (now called The Hub). Kath wanted it to be ten couples in a smaller room. So Pastor Dave met with me to talk about it up in Desert View—a really nice room they had upstairs. We even laid out tables. He said, "I think you need to keep it to around fifteen tables . . . keep it smaller the first time . . . in case something unforeseen happens." When I got home, I told Kath we'd go smaller, and she said, "Thanks for listening to Pastor Dave and not me!" She was right to say that, as my pride was getting in the way.

January 5, 2014, the classes started with sixty-one cou-ples. We had so many sign-ups, we planned another class starting three weeks after that one was to finish. Four of the table leaders were from my men's group. We had 97 per-cent attendance for the full six weeks, which is incredible. The Lord showed up big. And from that first class, a team of couples was formed for future classes. We had no idea what would happen in the years following; the Lord obviously did.

As we got closer to the end of the series in mid-February, Kath reminded me that part of the prerequisite for us being in marriage ministry and using The Art of Marriage material was to attend FamilyLife's Love Like You Mean It cruise. But it was *the day after* our series ended, and I did *not* want to go. I fought it. Going on a cruise was not high on my list. In fact, I said going to the dentist was a better option! Don't get me wrong, I like my dentist, but you know what I'm saying! We went, and it seemed as though we were the last couple to get off the boat. It was an amazing experience for our marriage, and the relationships we made were significant and lasting to this day. Honestly, that cruise was not only the biggest impact on our marriage, but also on the ministry and the calling God had for us.

I loved this cruise, and it wasn't about the places we went. It was a special time for Tim and me in that there was no one on the boat we knew, which was rare for us. Tim is so well known— everywhere we go people know him because of his presence in the community. But not there. It was so nice to meet new people together for the first time and really spend quality time together. We were especially excited coming straight from our first Art of Marriage study. Everything was still so fresh in our minds.

In Case You Were Wondering . . .
TIM

In my head, going on the Love Like You Mean It cruise felt like I was going as a prisoner, but I was committed to Kath. I didn't feel we needed any additional help in our marriage, as it was already in an awesome place. I made every effort to talk Kath out of it. After going, I realized it must've been Satan making me feel this way, as that first cruise ended up being one of the greatest investments we made in our marriage, along with the ministry we were leading. To this day we find as many ways as possible to invest in our marriage.

The cruise is also where we met Dennis and Barbara Rainey—FamilyLife's co-founders—and Dave and Ann Wilson—hosts of FamilyLife's radio program. We met the Raineys after talking with their daughter Ashley in the massage waiting area. She asked where we were from, what we did, and if it was our first cruise. When we said we'd just finished our first class with sixty-one couples using The Art of Marriage, and that in three weeks we were doing another thirty-six-couple session, she wanted us to meet her dad, who happened to be Dennis Rainey! When we all met, Tim and Dennis hit it off. Later, Dennis took Tim to the front of ship to watch session 5 of his Stepping Up video for men. After seeing just one session of the video and meeting Dennis, Tim was very excited to read the book Stepping Up. I had no idea the impact that book would have on Tim. It soon became its own ministry within the bigger picture of our marriage ministry. And as the Stepping Up ministry grew, Tim would invite me to attend week 9 as his special guest to address questions the men had about a wife's perspective of our journey. Once again God was stretching me.

This cruise was also the beginning of an amazing friendship with Dave and Ann. It was truly life-changing for us.

After we got home, it was evident and very clear that we had *finally* found our calling: marriage ministry! It became especially clear to us considering all we had endured and the transformation that had taken place after we put Christ at the center and started living for Him. The response we'd gotten from both times we led a marriage series left no doubt that there were a lot of other hurting couples who wanted and needed help—just like us—and we knew that if God could redeem our marriage, other couples could make it too, and that giving up was *not* the answer.

After decades of searching for ways of finding ourselves, then seeking and serving the Lord, we were ready to put even more focus into our calling now that we knew what it was. And to God be the glory with however He wished to use us, we were all in. We knew above all else we needed to be obedient to the Lord. No matter what.

Thoughts from the Kids . . .
JIMMY

Tricia, the kids, and I moved to South Carolina in the summer of 2013 for my work. In the spring of 2014, Dad mailed me a CD of the Stepping Up audio book. He called me to make sure I got it and told me I had to listen to it, as it is life changing. He suggested I put it in my car, as I had an hour and a half commute each way to work. To be completely honest, I didn't have any intention of listening to it. Every week or two Dad would ask if I had a chance to listen to it yet. I can't remember how many excuses I made up just hoping he would eventually forget about it. Some were pretty good ones, such as my new truck didn't have a CD player. Dad asked Tricia if she could put it on my iPod that I listened to music on. My father-in-law doesn't take no very easily!

One morning I was leaving my house for work around 4 a.m., and I hadn't even had a cup of coffee yet when my phone rang with Tim's name on my caller ID. It was 4 a.m. South Carolina time, which meant it was 1 a.m. in Washington where he lived at that time. My first thought was, "Oh no, something bad has happened for him to call me at this hour!"

I answered and said, "Hey Dad, everything all right?"

He said, "I figured you were on your way to work and called to ask if you've listened to the *Stepping Up* book yet."

I said, "Yes, I was driving but I hadn't had time to listen yet."

He suggested I take the next hour and half to listen while I was driving. He even said if I listened to the first chapter and didn't like it, he wouldn't ask me to listen to it again. I didn't have anything else to do for the next hour and a half, so I clicked on chapter 1 and started listening. When I pulled into the parking lot at work with the 3,500 other construction workers, I was a mess. Eyes red, tears down my cheeks, nose sniffling as I'm trying to collect myself and figure out what happened. You see, that morning on my drive, I felt the Lord speak to me through an audiobook. And Dad was right, it was life changing. It was the start of my journey that I'm still on.

WHAT ABOUT YOU?

Everyone, I mean *everyone* who is a follower of Christ, has a calling—a purpose bigger than themselves—yet many struggle to find it. They might serve in different ways in their church the way Kath and I did for years and still not figure out what it is. A calling *could* be your career, but most of the time, it isn't. A career is a vocation and a means of paying the bills and building a retirement portfolio. A calling is how and where God wants to use us to grow His kingdom. It has much more to do with serving Him and others than receiving something in return. It's important to be serving within our spiritual gifts. Do you know yours? Have you ever read 1 Corinthians 12 or Romans 12 where the Bible talks about the spiritual gifts? We all have them, and when we use them to serve God, we not only bless others, we experience joy and satisfaction unlike anything else.

Whatever is the case for you, one thing Tim and I learned that is key to discovering our calling was this: we searched and searched, and we didn't give up the search until we knew we'd found it. It's easy to get discouraged, especially when you face obstacles beyond your control, as we did. But it's so important to press on and keep believing He will guide your steps into the very place He wants you to be when He knows you're ready. In the meantime, He is at work developing qualities in you He knows you'll need for success. So don't ever give up. It's also important to know He does not call the equipped, He equips the called. The last thing I wanted was to get up in front of people and share all we had been through, but God had different plans.

QUESTIONS FOR TRANSFORMATION————————

- Finding our calling was so hard for us—it took us almost three decades of marriage to figure it out. During that time, we thought life was all about us and our happiness, which was self-centered.

- Do you know as a couple what your calling is? Are you sure? What are you doing to fulfill it? If you don't yet know, will you pray together—and keep searching—for God to show you what your calling is?

- Do you know your calling individually? If so, share with your spouse what you think it is. Are you in agreement, or is the jury still out?

- Are you interested in serving by yourself or as a couple? Why or why not? Talk together for three to five minutes about the strengths you see in each other that could benefit others, then agree to help and encourage each other in using them.

- How do you think it might impact your family or others if you were to find your calling and serve using your gifts?

My Radically Transformed Parents

Thirty-six years ago, two parents were faced with a choice, when the unexpected presented itself to them. I thank you both for embracing the unknown and taking a leap of faith and choosing each other and choosing me. When I was young, I know you both did your best with what you had. At that time, you were attempting things on your own, not even aware of what you were missing or that there was even another way. One thing that sticks out in my mind was your ability to work together and start from nothing and turn that into something that provided so much for our family. Memories that flood my mind are Little Caesar's at the old Tim Bush car lot, Sundays on the boat, family vacations, time at the lake in Tollgate, family snowmobile rides, playing cards together, my parents cheering in the stands at the football games while I cheered as a cheerleader, and many other memories. You filled my childhood with many experiences that will last a lifetime and be shared with generations to come.

When I was an adult, you both found what you had been searching for and missing for so many years. That something was Jesus and, oh boy, did He change you both! Watching how the Lord has transformed you both has been incredible and a privilege to get to witness. "Therefore, if anyone is in Christ, he is a new creation. The old has passed away; behold, the new has come" (2 Corinthians 5:17 ESV). God has radically transformed both of you and I am so blessed and thankful for the new parents that I have received in the process.

Dad, you have been my dad for thirty-six years, but these past nine-plus years have been the best. I know that we have had some growing pains during that time, but I will take all of it to get to where we are today. You are a true example of what it is to be a good husband, father, papa, leader, and friend. Thank you so much for the encouragement and love you've given to Jimmy. It is a gift knowing that he has you as a mentor. Thank you for pouring into him. I enjoy our time together, Dad, especially our coffee dates. Your words of encouragement and gift of time mean so much to me. I also want to thank you for the investments you make into your grandkids, and especially your time with our boys. Knowing that you are pouring into them and praying for them means the world to me. It takes more than myself and Jimmy to raise God's future generations and having a mentor like you is so valuable to me. Thank you for always speaking truth, for your prayers, for your love, your leadership, and your faith. I also want to thank you for sharing Mom with me. I know she is your crown jewel. Thank you for being a great husband to her and for loving her. I love you, Dad.

Mom, I truly love what our relationship has become. It took some trials and work to get here, but that was all worth it to arrive where we are. You are a Titus 2 woman and such a great example for myself, for Kaylene, and for so many other women. I love how you support me, speak truth into my life, pray for me, the way you love my husband and encourage and support our marriage, and for your gift of time. Whether we are talking on the phone (which we do a lot!), spending time visiting and drinking coffee, shopping together, or just being together, I value our relationship. You tell me the truth when I need to hear it and you encourage me. I love that you are my mom, my friend, and my sister in Christ. I also want to thank you for your relationship with Kaylene. She loves you so much, and it gives me great joy to watch that relationship grow. I value your mentorship in her life and the truth you give her. Thank you for being a huge part of our village and for supporting me and our family. I love you, Mom.

Thank you both for the gift you are as my parents. Thank you for loving Jesus and sharing this love with me and with all of us. I wanted to write this to both of you together because you go together so well. I know it wasn't always easy, but I thank you from the bottom of my heart for not giving up on each other and for your perseverance. God has made it so good! I am who I am because of my Heavenly Father, but also because of my two radically transformed parents. I love you both. Thank you from the bottom of my heart.

Love,
Your daughter, Tricia

Tribute written by Tricia and presented to Tim and Kathy on Christmas, 2018.

19

God Makes All
Things Good

*For we are his workmanship, created in Christ
Jesus for good works, which God prepared before-
hand, that we should walk in them.*

EPHESIANS 2:10 ESV

O nce Kath and I fully realized that our calling was in helping marriages—after about fifteen months at Bethel—we got the nod from Pastor Dave, with Kelli Temple- ton as our ministry lead. It was the fastest-growing ministry in the church. We did thirteen six-week classes—three a year for the first two years, then two a year after that. After the first class had sixty-one couples, which showed the need, we averaged thirty- to thirty-six couples each class. There were six to seven leader couples and usually one or two walking alongside us in training during each class. We were amazed at the overall response and how quickly the ministry grew.

One thing that stood out to us is that so many couples told us they had never heard another couple share such candid details about their marriage problems without shame in a church. By us sharing our story, other couples received hope that if we could make it, they could too. Women came up to Kath and asked to talk and share and pray. Men came up to me to do the same.

From our marriage classes, other leader couples began to lead marriage oneness, pre-marriage (which previously ran on its own), Art of Marriage Connect, and Vertical Marriage, plus mentoring couples outside the classes. We held many large events as well, and all of it was beginning to stir another change in me.

Thoughts from the Kids ...
TRICIA

Jimmy and I got the privilege of serving on the ministry team with my parents at Bethel for a few years. We served as table leads in Art of Marriage, we facilitated a Marriage Oneness class, and even put on an Art of Parenting class. It was really cool to see my parents using their story of brokenness to encourage others in their marriages. I have been to classes before where the leaders appear to be perfect people and it makes it hard to connect with them. My parents had been through it all and God had redeemed their marriage. This gave them a unique perspective that many could relate to in some way or another. It was almost like if God can fix that then everyone has a chance!

As Kath and I got more involved and focused on our calling and marriages, I began to feel torn between wanting to do more ministry and working at the dealership. Our boys were my business partners, and I had a growing concern I wouldn't be able to carry my part of the load and be so involved in ministry. I started to feel like the car business might not be conducive to how life was changing, but in that thinking, I would need to sell our dealership. It was not easy to even think about—it's what I'd done for so long. Plus, owning a BMW dealership is like reaching the pinnacle in the car business. When you have one, you've literally "arrived" in the car business—it doesn't get much better! Plus I would be taking away part of my boys' livelihood and ability to take care of their families. In addition, one son was having some health issues; although he was still coming to work, and the other was working long hours. It helped that we remained closed on Sundays, but even so, long hours were the nature of the business. You did what you had to do. I felt conflicted!

I talked with another dealership owner from Portland named Ralph who was interested in buying the store. We connected in so many ways—our histories, our long marriages, and we were both driven. The main difference was, he was much more of a gentleman in his younger years than I was. He loved the business like I did, and when he came to see the dealership, he said a funny thing to me I've never forgotten: "I've owned close to thirty car dealerships in my career, and this one has a peaceful feeling I've never felt at another store."

He made an offer, but the money just wasn't good enough. But looking back, no matter what the offer was, it wouldn't have been good enough. Deep down, I wasn't quite ready, and Blake said that if we sold, he'd not be my son anymore. He was already enduring enough—he was going through a divorce. His wife didn't care for his new "believer" lifestyle. Kath and I were heartbroken about it, as none of us believe in divorce. So I declined Ralph's offer.

As I watched all of this unfold, I could tell that Tim struggled with balancing work and our ministry. The dealership was getting more and more in the way. I knew for certain it was time to sell when I attended one of Tim's last sales meetings—he wore his love for Jesus on his sleeve. He had his Bible and as he read Scripture to his employees, I knew right then that he needed to get out and we needed to do more ministry.

The nagging feeling of wanting to be free to focus on ministry stayed with me ever since I talked to Ralph, and by Christmastime, God made it clear what He wanted me to do.

Kath and I were at our cabin on Christmas Eve getting ready to celebrate together when my phone rang. It was Richard, the BMW representative.

"Tim, I've been calling your store all day, and nobody is answering."

"Yeah, well, we're closed."

"What do you mean, you're *closed*?! Christmas isn't until tomorrow, and you're a BMW dealer."

"Richard, I told all of the employees that if we hit all our numbers by the twenty-first of the month, everyone could take five days off, and that includes the day before Christmas Eve, Christmas Eve, Christmas Day, and the Sunday and Monday after that."

He flew off the handle: *"It's inappropriate to run your business like that!* Even though you've hit all your numbers, you need to be there for your *customers!"*

"Well, I need to be there for my employees, too, Richard." And with that, things became very clear. When we hung up, I called Ralph.

Suddenly the money didn't matter to me anymore—I needed to sell. Ralph was willing to stand by the previous deal we had discussed, and I was ready to sign. We closed our deal, and it was all sold on April 6, 2015, except for one thing . . . the Fruit of the Spirit paintings. Those we kept, and they hang with joy-filled memories in our home to this day.

And I should say, Blake is still my son. We are closer than ever, he is married to Cara, and they share two of the youngest of our eight grandkids, Collins and Wilder. And Ralph? He and I have become great friends too. We talk often, Kath and I still buy and service our cars with him, and I've had no seller's remorse.

Thoughts from the Kids . . .
CARA

I have only known Tim and Kathy since after God completely transformed their lives. When I entered their world, in 2016, it was through their son, my husband Blake. With only a month and a half of dating before Blake proposed and then married three months later at their lake house, there was little time to really get to know them or their story, but we made the most of the time we had. One thing remains constant and that is that they have consistently been on fire for the Lord and their marriage ministry. The time we did spend together during those short months before the wedding, it was crystal clear that they were very excited for Blake to marry a woman that loved the Lord and have a marriage that honored God. So much so that Kathy sent me a text message about how excited she was and that she also wanted us to keep in mind all that it entails (mostly not having sex before marriage). What a BOLD but special message, I immediately thought. Blake and I had already had that talk, but knowing she cared enough about me in that short time to try and protect my heart and relationship with her son is something I will always cherish.

———

Selling the dealership set us free to focus more on helping marriages, and by the winter of 2019, the ministry had twenty-two couples leading classes of all kinds. Things were constantly happening in marriages at Bethel—so much so that we became known as the church that invested in marriages like no other in Tri-Cities.

Before leaving Bethel, Kath and I finally got to hold a one-day Art of Marriage event in The Hub—the same hub I wanted to start the ministry in—which packed the room with well over one hundred couples, plus the leadership couples. We'd been doing one-day events at other churches, but this was our first one there. It was significant for us because it would be the last marriage event we would hold at Bethel.

During all of this time, God didn't stop using us in other ways. As Kathy mentioned earlier, when I met Dennis Rainey on the cruise, he gave me a copy of his book *Stepping Up*, and it literally changed my life. Pastor Dave led our men's group in the hospitality room through a ten-week man-up study based on the book. Then at Kath's strong urging, after the first round of Stepping Up, it became apparent that the classes were yet another way to reach marriages through the men. And all of it started from a conversation on a ship with my friend Dennis Rainey and reading his book. The Lord knew to get us together—He had a plan for us not only as brothers in Christ, but as friends and Dennis as a mentor. He's even been involved with the writing and support of this book. I think it's cool how God puts the right people in your path for His purposes.

The more marriage ministry we did, the more I saw how much guys needed and wanted more than just the classes we led. I also saw how Tim loved speaking into guys' lives. I began to strongly feel that in order to get deeper with those men, Tim would need to go upstream with them, so to speak, and that's exactly what he did. He built a strong men's leader team and started sharing the R-rated version of his story, and it really got their attention. We saw so many lives change. They've told Tim story after story about how their and their sons' lives were being changed. He'd come home at night after leading the group super charged. I was and still am so proud of him.

Thoughts from the Kids . . .
AMANDA

We attended the iMarriage summer event at The Living Room, and I still use the tools we learned. I attended one of the first Art of Marriage classes at Bethel, served on the marriage team for day events, Vertical Marriage, Weekend to Remember, the Love Like you Mean it Cruise. We would have done none of this if our parents hadn't spurred us to.

We knew their story, even lived through some of it. It has been beautiful to watch these two people completely be vulnerable, share their hearts and not be ashamed. God has been using them and their story to transform marriages, broken relationships and build His Kingdom. I remember people asking me, "Isn't weird that you're here at marriage events with your in-laws talking about your marriage and sex!? I would laugh and just say, "No, not at all!" (Tim and Kathy were in the labor and delivery room when I delivered our first-born, so there's not much that is off the table).

As the ministry kept growing, I decided to build a building to use as a man cave—decked with all my favorite things and designated areas to hang out in. I called it the War Room. At the start it was used to put all my man stuff and some really cool cars—the kind you don't touch. But the Lord soon had different ideas, and it didn't take long for Him to make it clear that the War Room was to be used for ministry. As big as our church was, to get a room for ten weeks was nearly impossible unless we met at six in the morning. The only option I could see was to use the War Room to do the Stepping Up series and hold other ministry gatherings at the church.

Leadership had even talked about developing another area, mainly for marriage and family ministry, but it never got past the thought stage.

So in 2017, the War Room hosted the first of many one-day *and* ten-week Stepping Ups—there were too many to count. The band of leaders grew to an amazing number. There was a core of seven to ten dudes who rocked in ways only God could make happen by cooking and cleaning as well as discipling outside of the War Room. Those guys never ceased to amaze me in that they took on the challenge to be better husbands, better dads, better mentors . . . better men. I'll never forget the impact *they* had on *me* as well as so many others!

In Case You Were Wondering . . .
KATHY

God calls us to many things in life, not just one thing. But for us, God took us through a broken marriage and redeemed it to share with other couples to give them hope. This is what we are called to. I knew through Stepping Up and Tim connecting to the men, marriages could be healed. That's exactly what happened. The War Room was a special place.

While I was leading Stepping Up with the leader dudes, Kath and I continued doing more marriage series plus one-day events across the country. By January 2020, we wanted to do a one-day event using FamilyLife's The Art of Marriage material for couples at the church—it was something that had

never been done there before. Leadership wasn't as enthusi-
astic about this as we were, saying they didn't think people
would be interested in a one-day event, given we'd done so
many of the six-week version. We kept pressing the idea and
by February we moved forward with it, with well over one
hundred couples in attendance! This again shows the incredible need for and desire to get help and invest in marriages.

Even with this success, we soon found ourselves faced
with the same obstacle as other churches across the world:
COVID. As we all know, churches everywhere shut down. No
one knew what this virus was, only that it could be deadly—
not only to individuals, but to church bodies as well. There
were such conflicting sides people took that resulted in divi-
sion, and this included Bethel. Leadership didn't want me to
do a men's group or Stepping Up that spring because of all
the unknowns, and I understood that and said "Okay," so we
cancelled Stepping Up and shut down the War Room, which
had been so transformational in my life and others. But then
I started getting phone calls from the men in the group and
from men who had attended the R-rated version of Stepping
Up and our marriage events. They knew the part of my story
when my life looked so bad, I had thoughts of suicide, and a
handful of these men were having a growing number of similar thoughts. I *really* felt the need to be meeting with them, as
well as others who were calling. I felt that if I didn't, I would
be in disobedience to the Lord. I felt driven by pure compassion and nothing else. I set up phone calls with my leader
men and a few others on a weekly basis and found a lot of
unrest going on—I was honestly having some myself. Prayer
requests were constant for so many—the phone calls were
ramped. Over a six-month period, I received seven calls from

men asking how I felt when I thought of suicide, which troubled me.

I called Pastor Dave, who had been retired a few years by that time. He still led the Tuesday morning men's group, and he was also sheltering in place. I expressed to him how much I thought the men still needed to meet regardless of the circumstances and that we could meet at War Room so the church wouldn't be compromised. He admitted he was getting similar calls, so he agreed. We told the guys they could wear a mask or not—everyone was welcome. But when the elders got wind, they asked me to stop meeting there. They wanted us to meet at the church with masks and sit outside six feet apart. So out of respect for them, we did as they asked for three weeks . . . and *no* one liked it. It was very uncomfortable and not close like we used to be. Some of the guys even said they wouldn't come anymore.

After going back to the elders about it, we finally came to a head: they not only wanted us to stop meeting, but they also wanted me to quit meeting with men altogether and follow the governor's lockdown order. They said not to worry about the guys but to follow their lead as they were trying to keep people alive; what I was doing was against their leadership.

This was a defining time for me. I believe in being a team player—we'd all been in the trenches together over eight years—but also believe in being obedient to what God tells us to do. And for me, this felt like a matter of obedience. I was also seeking wise counsel from several men I looked up to across the country.

After praying, I shared in a Zoom meeting with the leaders. From my heart, I recapped how we'd served together in so many capacities. I told them how much I loved them all.

But I couldn't let it go—I was going to keep meeting with the men. I then reiterated everything I'd said in an email to them. About ten days later I received their response: all my leadership in the church was taken away. They simply thanked me for the things I'd done, and they made no mention of Kath or her leadership, not a word. It really broke our hearts, but we at least had peace in our brokenness because it was a matter of obedience, not self-will. We are responsible for our obedience, but the consequences are up to God.

In Case You Were Wondering . . .
KATHY

I continue to learn that being comfortable is not what God calls us to. Life was getting sweet and comfortable serving in our calling. Then COVID . . . God taught me so much through this time. He took us out of our comfort zone, and we continued to follow God, not man. This can only happen through maturity in Him. God continues to be faithful, and we continue to enjoy the journey. It's not always easy but it's all worth it. God has taken us places I would have never dreamt of.

In Case You Were Wondering . . .
TIM

In my understanding of God's Word, He created marriage before the church, so why do churches have divorce care and no marriage ministry over other ministry options? This has been a constant thought for me to ponder. I'm so thankful for the leaders that caught the vision.

—————

If you've been a Christian for even a short time, you've probably heard Romans 8:28: "We know that in all things God works for the good of those who love him, who have been called according to his purpose." This promise was true for us. By August 2020, some churches were beginning to open, so we were on our way to do a marriage event in North Platte, Nebraska, when the president of Family Life, David Robbins, called. He had become a friend and marriage ministry partner soon after we'd met. He said, "Tim, why don't you and Kath officially make War Room Ministries a nonprofit? Do your own thing in marriages and with the men, and even become a FamilyLife affiliate staff member? We will support you spiritually, with prayer, with our resources, and we'll honor what you're doing for the Lord and what He's doing through you."

Kath was listening as David spoke, and immediately after I hung up, she said, "This is an answer to prayer!" She was excited with me for the first time in a while. The event in Nebraska was a home run for the Lord, with thirty-seven couples investing in their marriages.

When we got home, I went to the War Room and took out most of the cars—even sold some of my favorites—to make more room not only for men, but for couples' meetings as well. I kept leading Stepping Up and it literally became a whole new ministry with over *three thousand guys* going through it. The Lord also opened one-day opportunities all over the country, as far east as Orlando, Florida, and many other places. We have relationships from many of these places still going strong.

As of today, Kath and I have continued holding one-day conferences all over the United States using The Art of Marriage material. We also continue to be open to what God has for us in impacting marriages for Him. When I look back, I can see that what happened during COVID could have been meant for harm, but God used it for our good, as well as the good of all the men (and women) who are seeking to make their marriages stronger and united with Christ. *To Him be the glory!*

Thoughts from the Kids ...

When my parents were stripped of their leadership at Bethel, it rocked our whole family. Jimmy and I had attended Bethel for most of our marriage. And not only did we attend, but the entire family did too. It was such a blessing to worship together as a family, most times sitting together during service. Ultimately, we ended up leaving the church and experienced lots of church hurt. We know that a church is made up of imperfect people and that can happen, but it was a hard time. The last couple years we have been mourning the loss of what we had. We even tried to go back and visit but realized it wasn't the same. I am truly thankful though for the several years we had together all worshipping under one roof and often serving together as well.

Tricia

WHAT ABOUT YOU?

Once Tim and I dove all the way into marriage ministry, our energy, focus, and momentum really took off. It was and remains so rewarding to be able to help others and be affirmed in the process. At the same time, we realized we needed to step away from anything that held us back, including the dealership, which had been his life's work. Letting go was hard, but he had to choose between being all in or having a foot in each lane and trying to manage both. I'm glad he chose ministry. I've learned that being a full partner with your spouse in ministry is truly a gift and something that took us—with the Lord's help—around thirty years to achieve. We're a living testimony that God is never finished with us. He has truly taken our mess and made it our ministry.

Along our journey, Kath and I also realized that to be used by God in marriage ministry, we had to fine-tune and live out what we were leading in our own marriage. Otherwise, how could we possibly speak into other people's lives with integrity? Can you identify? As God led us—and is possibly leading you—into our calling, He took us through several seasons of building and equipping us so that our marriage could withstand the pressures that come with being in ministry. And that's why sometimes it takes time to discover our callings—we are growing in Him all the time. Plus, we can have many callings in life, not just one. Through life's seasons, our callings can change as long as we're investing and growing with Him at the center. This is why I love Philippians 4:13: "I can do all things—[*all of His callings*]—through him who gives me strength" (emphasis added).

QUESTIONS FOR TRANSFORMATION————

- As we mentioned before, our hearts were broken when we left Bethel—our church home for over nine years. Church hurt is very real and can happen to anyone. Have you ever had a church hurt? If so, share with each other what your stories are, as they are probably different. Even if you experienced hurt together, your feelings and experiences might vary. Have you been able to extend forgiveness? If it's still a sensitive subject, will you ask the Lord right now to heal your hurt?

- If you are serving in any capacity, do you feel supported by leadership in what you are doing? If so, have you thanked them for their support? If you aren't getting the support you need, will you tell them and commit their response to prayer?

- One thing we did before deciding to keep meeting with the men in group was to seek wise counsel. If you ever needed wise counsel, who would you reach out to? (It would need to be someone of the same sex as the one who's seeking.) Will you share with each other who it might be?

- How did your church handle COVID? Have you forgiven your leaders for any mistakes they made in your eyes? It might be time to ask God now in prayer to reveal anything you've not dealt with and seek healing through forgiveness.

20

Put a Stake in the Ground

*Therefore, preparing your minds for action, and being
sober-minded, set your hope fully on the grace that will
be brought to you at the revelation of Jesus Christ.*

1 PETER 1:13 ESV

When Kath and I got saved, we had no idea what God had in store for our lives as a married couple. All we knew was that we didn't do a very good job until He came into the picture, and we put His way of doing things above our own. Out of His love for us, He not only saved us for eternity's sake, but He also rescued us from the messes we'd made and put us on a completely new path of living for Him. We haven't looked back—into our old lives, that is. But looking back over our new life together, we have still made mistakes—not because of selfish ambition, but because we're human. We're imperfect. You don't become a Christian and suddenly everything's perfect. That's quite a switch in thinking, considering that the first ten years of our marriage I thought I was perfect!

In Case You Were Wondering ...
KATHY

I remember the hunger I had for God and His Word. I am still hungry and know God has a lot more work to do in me. If you're a believer and not in God's Word every day, first I would say you are missing out on so much. It is a privilege to be able to have His Word to read. The only thing that will change us is His Word. It is alive and living. You have read our story, so don't wait. Give your life to Jesus. This is why you are here on this earth. He created you and loves you. He has a purpose for you. He wants to spend eternity with you, and so do I. If our story has brought you to Him, I look forward to our eternity together. Come say hi!

Seriously, though, that night on December 21, 2009, when I looked down at Kath and said, "Everything's going to change," it did. We've still disagreed and even argued at times, but the way we work through conflict is completely different, all because Christ is at the center. He's got to be at the center of all that we do, because we know we're capable of slipping back into old patterns. Which brings me to what I call *putting a stake in the ground*. Before I go further on this, I want to say that while this is important for wives to do, I think it is especially important for men to lead in their marriage. When I get the privilege to do what I call a man-up talk, one of my main points is that it took me forty-seven years to become a man, even a successful one in the world's eyes let alone as a Christian. The way I lived was childish in so many ways, and my "because I said so" mentality was no way to love my wife, who is one of the Lord's daughters. Now I like to challenge other men, so they'll learn these things earlier in their marriage rather than later like I did.

I believe it's vital for every couple to put a stake in the ground. When I say this, I mean being intentional about how you're going to live—beginning with completely turning away from your old life and what you used to do before Christ and living in a way that honors God. If you say you're walking with the Lord, you've got to put stakes in the ground that define what you're going to do differently. When you move from believing in God to making God the Lord and Savior of your life and repenting from your old way of life— that's the first stake you've put in the ground. From there, you add more stakes that create clear guidelines for a husband and wife to thrive and grow closer in marriage. Husbands must be on board that they're going to live bigger than themselves and be leaders in this. You must have some goals in your marriage that are not only intentional, but also nonnegotiable.

For Kath and me, we put our first stake in the ground and have since discovered what we consider to be some of these nonnegotiables—they're our stakes that are driven deep down and will not be moved, no matter what. They are things we do intentionally every day to make a difference in our marriage and in our testimony as we live for the Lord.

When we were first saved and after we put our stake in the ground, after seeing all that God had done to that point, we

*couldn't not think and act differently about things. Learning
what repentance is and that it's more than just confession; it's
about intentionally turning away from what you used to do. For
example, in my past, I didn't seek to have an affair, but I did put
myself in situations that catered to the opportunity with alcohol
and men. I drank and let things happen because I'd been drinking.
Now, I wouldn't even put myself in a situation like that in the first
place. Tim and I don't let ourselves get into settings that could
compromise our new way of living. When God starts changing
how you think, He changes who you are on the inside and puts a
different lens over your eyes to see clearly—the way He sees things.
It's all part of being intentional, of having a stake in the ground.*

What follows are eight of the stakes we have found helpful in establishing us in our relationship with the Lord and in
strengthening our marriage.

STAKE #1: READING GOD'S WORD

*Looking back, the Lord began moving in and preparing our hearts
for Him when we started reading Proverbs together. It didn't take
long that we felt and saw so much change in us. Reading God's
Word became part of our every day, no excuses. This happened
before we even had our stake-in-the-ground moment, which
shows you the power of God's Word. Our moments of conversion
solidified what we'd already been learning months before, which
then led to our first stake in the ground of turning from our old
way of life to doing everything God's way.*

*From that point, our commitment to reading the Bible every
day became an even more deliberate act, and we haven't stopped.
We continue to get up early and begin each day that we can with
reading His Word. If we're traveling apart, we're intentional to*

read on our own—the important thing is that we read it and encourage each other. It's important for believers to do this because we know firsthand that doing so can and will change how we view God, how we make decisions, how we think, how we act, and how we treat each other. His Word is filled with wisdom for living, how to handle conflict, what it means to love one another, and the purpose for our very being. As Christians, how do we know what God says about us and how to live if we don't read His Word? How do we get to know God and His purpose for us if we don't read His Word? God's Word is food for Christians. If we don't read it, we will starve and we will do what this world tells us to do—and the ruler of this world we live in is Satan. God's Word is the only *thing that can change us in a lasting way. I personally know this because I have lived it. God's Word saved me!*

It was February 10, 2012, when I started reading the One-Year Bible. I read it every day and went through it three times in three years. At that point I wondered if I should read something else, so I asked Pastor Dave, and he said to read a different version—just keep reading the Word. Of course, I listened to him because he modeled what he preached. Since the day I asked, he's read it twenty-eight times in twenty-eight years. He also encouraged Kath and me to go through a junior seminary class—Dave called it "seminary JV"—that the church offered, so we did. It was called Porter Brook and was a one-year commitment, but we didn't mind because we were so hungry to understand God and His Word.

Hebrews 4:12 says, "For the word of God is alive and active. Sharper than any double-edged sword, it penetrates even to dividing soul and spirit, joints, and marrow; it judges the thoughts and attitudes of the heart." This is so true because you can read a verse one year, then the next year read the same verse and it will come alive and speak something completely different to you, depending on what you're going through. It *never* stops speaking. I've read portions of Scripture and thought, *Wow! I've never heard this before!* Even though I'd read it twelve years in a row before then.

STAKE #2: PRAYER

Another stake in the ground—something we do every day, no matter what—is praying together. There is no right or wrong way to pray, it's simply talking to God. Tim started praying for us when he didn't even know how—he just did it. It took me time to pray out loud with him, but once I did, I haven't stopped. No matter how much or how little you've prayed, no matter how awkward it might feel at first, it's important simply to start. In the process of talking to God together, the wife hears what's on her husband's heart and the husband hears what's on his wife's heart—things they wouldn't otherwise learn.

Plus, our relationship with God grows through prayer, and He wants that. He is waiting to hear from all of us, to talk with us. A true friendship will never grow if two people don't talk to each other, and it's the same with God. Matthew 18:20 says, "For where two or three gather in my name, there am I with them." That's the beauty of praying together!

I believe you've got to be in God's Word every day to be connected to the Lord, but you've also got to be praying and inviting Him into your marriage. I've lost count of the number of guys—*hundreds* of guys—that have said to me, "So you pray *every day* with your wife? *Every day?!* How do you *do* that every day?!" As though they're astonished. That's like saying, "So you eat dinner *every day*? How do you eat dinner *every day*?!" This is one of the nonnegotiables for me, and I'm so glad Kath agrees.

When I started praying with Kath, I had no idea what I was doing, I just spoke from my heart. It doesn't have to be a formal, structured thing; just be real and honest from the heart. God doesn't care how eloquent your prayers are, in my opinion, just that you have an honest conversation with Him. It's important to model praying together for your kids and grandkids, your friends, and other believers with the hope that you're planting seeds by doing it yourself. This means you let them catch you in the act when they are with you. It's important to always be the same person with them as you are in private, no matter what. Otherwise, you can appear hypocritical and make them stumble. Strive to stay solid, and realize you are being watched.

I think of the time when we were at The Living Room— less than a year after I got saved—and at the end of a service Pastor Mel motioned from the piano for me to come forward and be there for anyone who needed prayer. Well, I didn't know how to pray—I mean, I *really* didn't know what I was doing—but I went. A guy who looked to be about seventy and walked with a cane came up and said, "Please pray for me." He didn't say what to pray for, he just asked me to pray, so I did. I don't even remember what I said, I just prayed, and he left.

Several months later during the iMarriage class Kath and I led, that same man and his wife were in attendance, and at a break he walked up to me and said, "I want you to know that the day I asked you to pray for me, I was considering ending things. What you prayed was exactly what I needed to hear." That's how the Holy Spirit works—not always when we know what we're doing, but when we're obedient to what He wants us to do, and He wants us to pray about *everything* without ceasing. On a side note, the guy has been a friend of mine ever since.

STAKE #3: SERVING THE LORD

Over the years before I got saved, it's clear that God was pursuing Kath and me, even to the point of different people speaking into my life about having a calling from Him. Then after I devoted my life to Him, the search to discover my calling became consuming through all the ways we served in the church. Kath and I went to every church service, but that's not the same as serving in the church body. In looking for my calling, I got involved in the FAT team, fundraising, looking for and buying property, remodeling, going to other churches with the pastors, taking classes, doing Bible studies, starting small groups, and ultimately doing marriage classes. Through the act of serving, we found out what our calling was and is: marriage ministry. Kath and I prayed about what our calling might be, but it was through serving in our church home that we found it. At times we thought other ministries we did could be our calling, and we certainly had gifts in some of those areas, but it wasn't until speaking into marriages and working with men—which Kath says is a direct way of getting to the marriages—that our true calling emerged. Sharing our redemption story was our "for sure" calling and it made sense—we had gone through so much. Why? To be used for His purpose in helping other couples.

On that note, I think *everyone* has a calling on their life. As Christians, God wants to use each of us to grow His kingdom. But a lot of people struggle, like Kath and I did, with knowing what their calling is, let alone getting over a "find yourself" mentality. It takes intentionality to discover your calling, and it was another stake in the ground, another non-negotiable for us. Even when our own family disconnected from us for a while, we couldn't *not* be involved in our church home. It's through serving and growing in our faith that we were eventually led into where God wanted us to focus our gifts and talents and experiences. After all, if our marriage could survive despite all we'd been through, other marriages could—and have—as well. God knew that and had a plan all along to use us to help others. But we had to figure this out.

I think of Matthew 6:31–33: "Do not worry saying, 'What shall we eat?' or 'What shall we drink?' or 'What shall we wear?' For the pagans run after all these things, and your heavenly Father knows that you need them. But seek first his kingdom and his righteousness, and all these things will be given to you as well." While Jesus is speaking in reference to physical needs, you could easily apply this to say, "Do not worry, saying, 'What shall we do?' or 'How shall we serve?'" Just seek Him, just serve Him as He leads, and He'll orchestrate circumstances that lead up to your calling—not the world's calling but His, and they're often not the same.

For me, as I kept studying the Bible and serving by leading my own studies, helping to launch small groups, going with Tim to seminars and leading that first marriage series . . . as God continued to work in my heart and my continued obedience to Him, a lightbulb finally went off about our calling: working and serving in marriages! And it turns out that it was.

By serving, I grew in my faith and became more and more confident about doing things I would never have done otherwise.

Going to Rwanda without Tim, speaking with Tim in front of crowds, leading devotions in front of people—I don't think any of these would have happened without active involvement in the church and the encouragement I received, as well as the opportunities that came up. For us, serving God, serving our community, serving each other is another stake in the ground that will remain no matter what. We were turned inward—into ourselves—for so long. But God did not create us to be isolated or self-focused. That is our tendency in our sin nature.

Another thing we've experienced since serving others is that when Tim and I serve together, we've grown closer in our marriage. Having a shared purpose has brought us together in ways we never realized were possible. Our hearts are full when we serve together.

STAKE #4: BOUNDARIES IN CHURCH AND MARRIAGE

One thing I discovered not long after we started serving in the church was that we didn't know where and when to stop—or at least Tim didn't. There wasn't anything he said no to, and we started fighting about it. I even think there was some ego involved. He went from Tim Bush in the community to Tim Bush in the church, and that's not the right motive for serving.

I was so frustrated because Tim was working the dealership with seventy employees while he spent at least twenty-five hours a week on FAT items. Then there were the fundraisers, launching small groups . . . the needs were so great, and they seemed to be overtaking us. In the meantime, I was more concerned about Tim's relationship with God. I wanted him to do more studies and learn more about Jesus with me. That was when I told Pastor I didn't feel like Tim was making me a priority anymore. And Mel said, "You and Tim need to realize that the church is not your relationship with God. They are two different things. It's more important to have a relationship with God than to be at church all the time."

After that, I finally put the brakes on the amount of time Tim spent, and he listened—something he wouldn't have done before. We decided together that we needed to have some boundaries. And as we went full bore into marriage ministry, we had to establish even more boundaries for the health and safety of our own marriage. For example, we give our phone numbers out at conferences for anyone who wants to reach out, but we make it clear, if you're a woman, don't call or text Tim, call me. And if you're a man, don't contact me, call Tim. Our history of infidelity has made us even more aware of how affairs can and do happen. Even in the church. Tim and I have put up hedges to protect our marriage. We both know we have a target on our backs, so we guard all we do and say to honor each other so that our marriage stays pure.

Yeah, it's so important to have strong boundaries within marriage so there is no gray. They must be very clear, with no question in either person's mind about what's okay or not. When I talk to guys, I tell them that if they see me with someone of the opposite sex and she's not my wife, they have permission to embarrass me by walking up and asking me which one of my family members it is. If it's not my wife, point it out in front of everyone.

I also won't ride in a car with someone of the opposite sex without Kath unless they're family. For wives, even being with your pastor one-on-one should be a caution because they don't always have good boundaries. It's not necessarily their fault—they serve their flock, regardless of gender.

But perception can be reality to people in lots of ways, and a wrong perception can turn into gossip. Bottom line, it's important not to leave anything to the imagination, to have good boundaries. No exceptions!

STAKE #5: ACCOUNTABILITY

Every marriage needs nonnegotiables—every couple must have them, in my opinion. It could be one, it could be ten, and they should be established based on who you are, your backgrounds, your weaknesses, your stories, and the experiences you've had. It's very important to have people in your life who will hold you accountable for your actions and decisions, especially if you're going through a difficult time in your marriage. I like to lead other men in this because I understand the importance of it, given my background.

Kath and I have open access to each other's phones and computers. This also brings me to the topic of pornography, which is very prevalent everywhere, even in the church. Statistics show that up to 60 percent of churchgoing men look at porn, and I'd bet the number is higher with the internet and all the easy access that just pops up. Pastors and leadership are part of the church too, and almost 40 percent of women are also involved in porn at some level. The numbers and surveys vary, but the point is, it's a problem, and very few churches are addressing it with accountability of any kind. If that isn't available in your church, find a few others you can turn to—other believers who will be forthcoming—and meet regularly for accountability's sake. This is why I've led the Stepping Up ten-week class and a one-day class based on Dennis Rainey's book. Guys have got to be able to have conversations with other guys, and not just about tempta-tions. If one guy tells me he has marriage problems, I don't just listen to what he thinks is wrong with his wife; I ask what part of the problem is *him*! I've found that most men blame their wives for their problems before looking at themselves. But once they talk to a man that gets it and digs deeper into them, they can start being accountable for the part they might own. That's what good accountability groups provide. Proverbs 27:17 says it well: "Iron sharpens iron, as one man sharpens another" (NLT).

Accountability is a non-negotiable for me. If there isn't a group available, I'll start one. There's no excuse. As I'm writing this, Kath and I are in the process of moving, and the hardest thing for me to leave is my men's accountability group. But you can trust that it won't be long before I start another group in our new city.

For me, I need to be around other women who love Jesus. This isn't easy because I'm such an introvert, I tend not to care for women's groups or even large women's conferences—I'd rather be with Tim. But it's so important not to isolate yourself. I make it a point to meet with other women regularly who inspire me to grow in my faith and share about similar issues we have for encouragement. It's good for me to learn from them, and in some cases with younger women so we can learn from each other. I hold Bible studies in my home, not because I want to but because it's good to have that connection and fellowship. I am getting bet-ter with being intentional about making women friendships and have developed some very special ones. The older I get, the more important I see this is and that the rewards are so special.

And now . . . the topic that seems to get a lot of attention at our conferences!

STAKE #6: SEX

Yes, Tim and I have a stake in the ground about sex. One of the keys is intentionality—not in just the act, but in all that leads up to it. Most men can have sex on demand, but women must be intentional about even thinking about it. Sex starts in a woman's brain, so that means we must begin preparing for sex by thinking about it. And why wouldn't we? Sex is a gift from God within the boundaries of the marriage covenant. It's meant to be as enjoyable for wives as it is for husbands, yet so often it gets a bit complicated, which is why it's important to talk about it. That is the first step toward being intentional with the act. Communication is critical.

Speaking to women now, I'll be candid, there are some women who don't like it, so if that's the case, I think it's important to find out why. Again, it's a gift from God—He made women to have sex, among other things—but as with all gifts, it's not a gift unless it's received. If there is a physical reason that holds you back, see a doctor for help. If there's an emotional block, it's worth the effort to figure out why, even if it means counseling for yourself or with your husband. I know Tim wants to feel wanted and desired, and sex creates closer connection, just as much for me as it does for him.

If you do enjoy making love with your spouse, this is where communication can make it even better. Our husbands can't read our minds. We need to tell them what we like and need from them. Maybe even show them. There are so many resources now about different techniques and answers to questions. The important thing is to be intentional in talking about it together so you both experience what God intends on the most intimate level of your marriage.

My first thought to the guys about sex is, you can't fix your marriage problems in the bedroom—they must be fixed *outside* the bedroom! I spent years thinking our marriage would be fixed by having sex. (Remember my assumption before the wedding that frequent sex with Kath would end my wandering and solve everything?) She and I would have a fight, then once we had sex, I'd think everything was fine and our problems were over. Then three months later in a counseling session Kath would bring up the argument and say it wasn't over at all for her. I needed to have sex to feel better, and I did, but it's not the answer to fixing problems.

Lovemaking also begins outside the bedroom. This is done by connecting emotionally with your wife, nurturing her, paying attention to her, and serving her in ways that matter to *her*. This is why I get up early and unload the dishwasher and do other things before Kath even gets up—it means a lot to her. Be intentional about taking some load off your wife, whether it's going to the store, washing the dishes, preparing or planning a meal, or cooking and cleaning up your mess when you're done. Just listen to what she needs and wants, then do your best to serve her in those ways. Serving your wife is a gift you will end up loving. It sure is for me—serving Kath is one of my greatest joys.

There's also the issue of being healthy physically so you're able to have sex. At times my weight was as high as 260–290 pounds, and that didn't help matters. It's important to do what you can, both of you, to be healthy so you're able to be and do your best. If you are dirty at the end of a long day at work, clean up. If you need a shave, do it. Kath taught me early on that if I wanted to be in bed with her and expected anything to be a possibility, I'd best be clean when getting in the sheets. Brush and floss your teeth, for heaven's sake, unless you don't like kissing. Kissing creates other feelings, in case you didn't know!

Kath and I didn't talk about sex for over thirty years of marriage, but now, we've learned it's very important to talk about. It's okay to say if or why you're uncomfortable; it's okay to say what you want and what you like; it's okay to talk about whatever may be inhibiting you and preventing you from experiencing the fulness of the pleasure God intended it to be. He created sex, He wants a man and wife to enjoy it, so talk about it, get excited for it, be intentional about it.

STAKE #7: STEPPING INTO YOUR SPOUSE'S WORLD

This is also about being intentional to learn your spouse and making a point to do the things they love whether you like it or not. This is what love does. It's about finding out more ways to serve your spouse in the way that matters most to them.

One example is the way Tim goes to the mall with me. I know he'd rather go to the dentist than to the mall. He likes his dentist, but you know what I'm saying! He knows I love shopping, so he'll drive me there, he'll find a chair or bench and drink coffee and . . . wait. When I'm done, he'll carry my bags to the car, and occasionally jokingly tell me I need intervention. But it's all done in love and fun. Tim does so many things with me that I know he has no interest in but does them because he loves me.

I know Tim likes to fish, so when he started talking about fishing in Alaska, I said I would go with him. He really was shocked. We stayed in a small, meager cabin, and the weather was freezing, but I went and didn't complain. I fished alongside him, and we had the time of our lives. This has become one of our favorite memories.

I also love driving more than the average person. When I want to drive somewhere and look at a property, or just simply drive, Kath will go with me, sometimes in the car, and sometimes in our motor home. I can drive 500 miles a day or more in that thing, even live in it if Kath would agree (she doesn't!). Since I love it so much, she rides with me without complaining.

Men, I want to say that, if your wife isn't happy in your marriage, it's your job to find out why. She needs to be treated like a gift, but even more than that, she needs to *feel* like one. If you're not treating her in ways that are important to her, you're not trying hard enough. What's wrong with getting her flowers for no reason (other than because she's a gift)? What's wrong with spending time doing what she likes to do? Whether it's shopping or hiking or eating at her favorite restaurant, serving her in the day-to-day stuff without her having to ask is so important. You may already do this, but I have found that most guys don't! Bottom line, you've got to wake up every morning and die to yourself. Ephesians 5:25 says, "Husbands, love your wives, just as Christ loved the church and gave himself for her." Well, Christ died for the church, so in the same way, if you want an amazing marriage relationship with lots of potential benefits, die to yourself, fellas. Don't do it for what you might get, do it because she's His daughter.

Be the man God wants you to be. It's not your job to make your wife happy, but based on Scripture it's your duty to love her and die for her. Can you do better? Are you leading her in a godly way? Praying for and with her? Reading and being in God's word? Never quit!

STAKE #8: LEAVING A LEGACY

One thing we all know that will happen to us in this life is, we're going to die. Yes, Christians have eternal life, but we'll leave our bodies on this earth, and when that happens, we can either be forgotten or we can live on through the generations after us. This is called *leaving a legacy*, and it's our final stake in the ground concerning our faith. Being intentional about how we can and will impact next generations is one of the most important things we can do. And I'm not talking about finances you leave your kids or grandkids. It's the spiritual torch you carry now that gets passed on to them. It's our chief aim to bring Jesus to them—our kids, our grandkids, our great-grandkids, and beyond. We may never even meet them, but they can meet Jesus because of the stake we put in the ground now. If we don't, who will have this influence?

One hundred years from now, no one will know us or have even heard of us, but God will know and use the things we do now far into the future that He has planned. Something we start today may not even be completed until after we're gone, and the next generation catches the vision and carries it on. That's okay if that's the way God wants to work His plan. Look at how God helped Abraham lead the Israelites to the promised land, only Abraham didn't inherit it. (See Acts 7:1–6.) The promise was fulfilled after he was gone. It's only one of many modeled Bible legacies we all reap from today.

This is my very heart: a hundred men could come into my life and every one of them could be an assignment from God, so I don't want to miss any of them. That's why I could never retire. A person can retire from their work and from making money, but we can't retire from our service to the Lord. It's all part of leaving a legacy. What will be yours?

One of the ways we can leave a strong legacy as Christians, as parents, as men, as women is to remain consistent and steady in our walk with Jesus. Our kids—adult children—and grandkids and everyone we come across in this life are watching everything we do. They're all watching whether we realize it or not. By the time our kids are grown, we can't tell them what to do (even though sometimes we try), so we are left to live out our faith without words but with our actions. Tim and I believe our actions, the decisions we make, and the ministries we serve in are what point people to Jesus, so they'll meet Him through us. Really, the way any of us live our lives is our legacy.

We can't be someone at church and someone else at home and someone else at work. Hebrews 13:8 says, "Jesus Christ is the same yesterday and today and forever," so if we're to be like Him, we need to have the same consistency today as yesterday and again tomorrow. Our everyday living—no matter what setting we're in—needs to be the same: a testimony for Jesus. The only way we can do this is if we're continually growing closer to Him and acting more like Him. This is a stake in the ground that should never be moved, no matter what. Another nonnegotiable—and one that people are watching all the time.

"Now to him who is able to strengthen you according to my gospel and the proclamation about Jesus Christ, according to the revelation of the mystery kept silent for long ages but now revealed and made known through the prophetic Scriptures, according to the command of the eternal God to advance the obedience of faith among all the Gentiles—to the only wise God, through Jesus Christ—*to him be the glory forever!*" (Romans 16:25–27 CSB, emphasis added).

In Case You Were Wondering . . .
KATHY

Marriage is a journey—one that is ever changing. Our marriage had to come to the surrender of ourselves to Christ. I believe to have a thriving marriage as God intended, all marriages must come to this point. Only with Christ in our marriage were Tim and I able to forgive each other for the terrible things we did. Only with Him were we able to build back trust. I want readers to know that as bad as things were, never was I in an abusive relationship. I would never advise a married person to stay in an abusive marriage—neither would I recommend divorce. Getting safe would be your first step. We serve a big God and as you see what He did in my marriage, He can do the same in any marriage.

In Case You Were Wondering . . .
TIM

Thinking about the importance of intentionality in everything I do, knowing that in how I love the Lord, love Kath, my family, and others, I could have an eternal impact on the next generation and potentially generations yet to come. When you think of what you do today and how it could have an impact on people or family you don't even know, let's just say it has a way to realign your thoughts. I've had to learn to think past myself.

WHAT ABOUT YOU?

Having a stake in the ground in what matters most provides clear and definitive guidelines within a marriage. It not only takes away the guesswork, but it gives us confidence in the way we live. There's safety in knowing what to expect from your spouse in certain situations that could otherwise cause insecurity and uncertainty. And there's comfort in knowing a decision's been made when we're faced with a potentially compromising situation—we can simply go to our stake and know what to do without second-guessing.

Having a stake in the ground also keeps us confident in our walk with the Lord. Knowing we're thinking and doing what would please Him—with consistency— brings His favor and a lot of inner peace and joy we wouldn't have otherwise.

What about you? You probably have stakes in the ground, but can you define what they are? Do they ultimately point your life to Christ through the way you live? Remember, others are watching— they're *always* watching.

QUESTIONS FOR TRANSFORMATION————

Cleaning the closet of your life is an important area for putting a lasting stake in the ground. Doing this can be hard—we know!—because it means that any secrets you have can impact the intimacy in your marriage now. But in the long term, planting these stakes can break you free for the most intimacy you've ever dream. Our friend Ann Wilson calls secrets "bricks," because in each area of your life that you leave something out or don't even talk about, a brick can form, and each brick can turn into a wall very quickly.

Satan gets a foothold in our lives one inch—or one brick—at a time. And when we give in to temptation, he "warms himself by this fire."[1] Don't let him be part of your marriage relationship.

Since there was a lot covered in this chapter, we've broken down the questions to address each topic.

1. What can you do to knock down any bricks in your relationship? Do either one of you have anything that needs to be said that has potential to keep you from the most possible intimacy? Do you have the freedom to share with each other, and, if so, can there be forgiveness? Pray about this together, then discuss each of these questions with honesty and grace, and remember, "Your biggest secret can turn into your biggest testimony."[2]

2. Do you have marriage goals, and if so, what are they? Set a time that you can be together without interruptions and

---

1. Thomas Watson, *A Body of Divinity* (Jay P. Green Sr., Lightning Source, 2002), pg. 94.

2. Devin Brewington [more specific source? I DON'T HAVE ONE.]

pray about what goals God would have you set. Then, individually, write five to seven ideas to share with the other. When you're finished, start with prayer again and share your ideas. Agree on the ones that are realistic and achievable considering your circumstances and, most of all, your hearts. Set up a follow-up time to talk about how you are doing. An example for this is when we decided to read five marriage books the first year, we had prayed and talked about the goal together. We only finished three, but did we fail or win?

Another example was to continue to pray together daily. We agreed without hesitation because we saw the difference it made in our marriage. Could this be a goal for you? What resources do you need to make it work? When can you do this? Where will it be? Make the time important by not being rushed or allowing phones or outside influences. The point is to make time and space to set your own goals to build your relationship.

To add one more: While working on completing your goals, try to come up with some nonnegotiables if you don't already have any. For Kath and me, as I touched on earlier, we don't ride with the opposite sex other than family in a car. We also don't meet the opposite sex other than family for coffee or lunch. Refer to the boundaries section in chapter 20, as this can be a nonnegotiable goal or a boundary, with certain exceptions depending on your family and acquaintances.

Speaking of boundaries . . .

3. What are some of yours? They can make your marriage affair-proof, so they should be important to you. List some together and be intentional about any more you can think of to add in the future.

4. What are your nonnegotiables? Can you think of one as a couple right now? Each of you come up with three to five that are important to you and bring them to your second goal-setting discussion. Also talk about how you will hold each other accountable when you are tested. Remember, there is no limit on these, as they are very important.

    Now about serving others . . .

5. How do you serve others? This is vital because doing so starts with each other. If doing formal ministry together is not your thing, what about you, the man, helping other men? Or ladies, how can you help other women? With the divorce rate being so high, could you even help one couple a year by agreeing to meet with them, listen to what they are facing, and pray for them each week? Be their encouragement? It's so important to get outside of ourselves and think of ways to serve others.

Thoughts from the Kids . . .
TJ

Mom and Dad's transformation is nothing short of a miracle straight from Jesus. I tell couples all the time that I know without a doubt they can make it in their marriage. And the reason is, my parents made it. Then they always look at me with confusion because most of them didn't know my parents before, they only know them now. Then when I tell them a little bit about their story, they just say, "You're talking about your parents that are married now?"

And I say, "Yup. Same ones. And if they can do It, I know anyone can." Without Jesus, you might be able to piece things together—heck It might even seem like everything Is working out most of the time. However, with Jesus, everything is possible.

21

Final Thoughts

Dear Readers,

Thank you for taking the time to read our story. Never once in it do we want to glorify our sin. As Tim stated earlier, my life verse is 2 Corinthians 5:17: "Therefore if anyone is in Christ, he is a new creation. The old has passed away; behold, the new has come" (ESV). This is true of us—we are not the same people. Tim and I both feel it's so important to share all that we did so you can see the big God we serve. He truly took us and our mess and turned it into our ministry. He can do this in any marriage.

I'm sure you wonder why we stayed together through all the years. Well, not one time of the twenty-seven years did we both want a divorce on the same day. This shows that if one is willing to fight for their marriage, God can work. God was always there with us because He knew so much more than we did. He had a plan.

Also, what we shared highlights so much trouble in our marriage, but I want to say that there were good times for us too—our kids would attest to this. In addition to the lows, our marriage was filled with many highs. The thing is, we both were searching for something better all the time. Looking back, I know this was God. He created us and put that on our hearts. We were stubborn for so long, but when He finally got our attention, He got it—and it stuck. I thank Him daily for this.

Our hope for you as you read this is that you will have hope for your marriage, if that's what you need. But even more, Tim and I want marriages to thrive and then turn outward to help others. We also want you to see that you cannot live in the dark with secrets and have a thriving marriage. In the end, the only lasting solution is for each of you to give your life to Jesus Christ and to put Him in the center. Repent and be saved, literally.

God designed marriage, and His plan is best. Don't wait as long as we did to surrender your lives and your marriage to Christ—He wants all of us. My hope is that this message is clear: make Jesus Christ your Lord and Savior! If we didn't, we would have missed out on all *the blessings we are experiencing now, including our eight grandkids. God is so good!*

Blessings,
Kath

Agreeing with Kath on everything is so very easy; all that she just said is 100 percent truth. Both Kath and I searched so long to find something that was already there right in front of us. We didn't have to go anywhere or buy anything; we just needed to commit to following Jesus and repenting of our old ways. It only took me forty-seven years to figure this out, but that shows it's never too late! My life verse—thanks to Jake Hill for leading me to it—is Psalm 37:4, "Delight yourself in the LORD, and he will give you the desires of your heart" (ESV).

Looking back at my life, even with all the challenges, there were many good things that happened. Mom fed me, she kept score at bowling and Little League games, she did the best she could in a tough situation. She also gave me up for adoption, which I'm totally thankful for. My Bush family name is something I'm very proud of. I even found out Pop's mom was a born-again Christian as told by his sister, Barbara, prior to her death. I only found this out a couple of years ago.

My grandparents raised me on their farm, and they taught me so many things, like loving and caring for animals, showing horses and other animals in 4-H. They gave me the opportunity to develop a love for music with many years of music lessons. The Lord ultimately used music for me to come to Him and give me the peace beyond understanding that only He can give.

My dad, George, and I reconciled many years ago and are not only friends, we love each other. He gets prayed for at least once a week when Kath and I pray for all our living parents and siblings. God made all things good between Dad and me—the painful things that happened so many years ago are totally forgiven.

With our Lord, *anything* is possible. Forgiving others and not carrying burdens toward them has been huge for me. But it took the Holy Spirit inside my heart to get to this place. The cool thing is being able to fully realize what Jesus did for me—for you—by dying on a cross. When I look back at my life, He took all the bad stuff and used it to build me into who I am in Him today. Hopefully my model now is something other men will consider adopting and passing down to coming generations. Cause if they do, it means Christ is using what comes out of me now for His good. To God be the glory!

Blessings!

Tim

Thoughts from the Kids . . .

Mom/Dad, Tim/Kathy have broken a generational cycle of sin in our family. They are there to support, love, and pray for us through our own struggles. All of us kids have in turn put time, effort, value and most importantly Christ into our marriages, which will have an effect on future generations. This doesn't mean that our family is perfect and never has problems, but our family will never be the same again. Jesus' grace was the only thing that made it possible for them to change. They went from having a marriage that was going to end in divorce to one that will last a lifetime because Christ is at the center of it. What a wonderful gift it is to have parents who fought so hard for their marriage and who will fight for mine and yours as well.

Love,
Jimmy & Tricia
TJ & Amanda
Blake & Cara

AFTERWORD

By David and Meg Robbins
President, FamilyLife

From raw brokenness to redemption.

From desperate despair to reconciliation.

From transformation to transforming others.

These are just a few of the themes and reasons we appreciate Tim and Kathy for taking the risk to share their story with vulnerability and candor . . . and the story and themes that are still being lived out. Knowing them, they don't seek to glory in the depravity of their journey, but to declare the glory of redemption and rescue found in Jesus. We hope it has inspired you to trust God for how He desires to work in your marriage. It may be hard to face and can sometimes be a long road, but God's faithfulness is trustworthy.

We met the Bushes just a few years ago after deep restorative work had been rooted in their marriage. In getting to know them, we were amazed to hear the places their marriage had been resurrected from, but we were even more amazed and interested in how God wanted to steward their story as a living legacy and trophy of radical grace to impact other marriages God brought across their path.

And we have cheered with joy and delight as God continues to steward Tim and Kathy's marriage and steps of faith to encourage others to trust in a very present God for a fresh work in their marriage. God invites each of us to participate with Him in declaring who He is in our corner of the world. Yes, even those—or perhaps especially those—of us who feel raw, desperate, and humbled.

God isn't looking for marriages who have it all together and look squeaky clean. It's the marriages who are doing difficult, formative work in their brokenness who can often best declare His healing power.

God doesn't necessarily want marriages who have prescriptive, polished plans and have the perfect outline to teach and impress. He flows through marriages who are increasingly surrendered and will respond to whatever and wherever God is leading them to next.

And God can certainly use the times we feel strong in our marriages to impact others, but He often gets more glory when we are trusting Him in the times we feel significant weakness and we respond in sincere dependence.

As 2 Corinthians 5:18–20 says,

> All this is from God, who reconciled us to himself through Christ and gave us the ministry of reconciliation: that God was reconciling the world to himself in Christ, not counting people's sins against them. And he has committed to us the message of reconciliation. We are therefore Christ's ambassadors, as though God were making his appeal through us.

Tim and Kathy are great examples of an imperfect couple desiring their marriage story to be a loud and resounding gospel message to the world around them. God is using their story of radical restoration to be ambassadors of Christ, helping others experience reconciliation in the challenging places people find their marriage.

And the invitation is for you too!

God created your marriage to live beyond itself. He desires your marriage to be a powerful conduit for the gospel. There are others struggling and hurting around you who are in need of safe spaces of belonging and encouragement. Maybe it's as simple as taking a step of faith to invite another couple over for dinner and hear each other's marriage stories, past and present. Maybe it's inviting some friends over weekly, for a month or two, for a marriage small group. Many people long for a place to talk about their marriage but often don't know where or how. Teaming together with your spouse in faith for something bigger than yourselves can bring greater intimacy in marriage. And as the Bushes' story displays, who knows where small steps of faith may lead!

We're hopeful for the ways you have been encouraged and inspired as you've read this book. Perhaps you've had honest, risky conversations with your spouse . . . Maybe some of them have gone well and some of them make you feel more stuck. One thing is certain, there is a God who is active and alive and at work in your marriage. He is worthy of our trust.

David and Meg Robbins

ACKNOWLEDGMENTS

First and foremost, thank You to Jesus Christ our Lord and Savior, who saved and redeemed us and our marriage for His purposes.

Thank you to our parents and grandparents for all the things you did right; even the imperfect things have been used for God's good. To the ones still living, we love and pray for you often. To the ones that have passed, you will be forever part of our story. Our redemption story could not have happened without all of you.

Thank you, Pastor Gedde. You were the difference we needed to make it through the first "near death" of our marriage. And thanks for being the first man to kneel with Tim in prayer.

Thank you to Ned Gosnell, who planted seeds and showed us another way. We're looking forward to seeing you in eternity and talking about how those seeds came alive. Thank you, Kate, for sharing Ned with us for the time we got—too short!

Thank you, Pastor Martens, for how you handled one of your first experiences at RLC with our daughter. You said you'd never had it happen before, and you did good. Thank you also for your friendship.

Thank you, Bill Voris, for taking a chance and telling us to search for our calling. It was great advice and something we know is having an eternal impact.

Thank you, Bob Kistner, for being a friend when we needed one so desperately and for really introducing both of us to the Bible. Your seeds planted have come alive in us both.

Thank you, Jake and Jennifer Hill, for being more than our counselors; you became friends, and the advice of us considering not to drink has borne fruit since August 31, 2009.

Thank you, Mel Haug, for introducing us to serving in the church and for baptizing us both August 25, 2010, for believing in us to do our first one-day event, for asking and supporting Tim to preach on 1 Peter 3:7 in both services, for leading Kath in Rwanda, and so much more. And thank you, Denise Haug, for being our friend.

Thank you, Monte Ingersoll and Suz, for the journey of building a church and traveling together as couples and ultimately remarrying us on Tim's fiftieth-birthday surprise in Mexico. What great memories.

Thank you to Deanne Stephens for leading us to The Living Room church where we found salvation.

Thank you to our first small group. You know who you are and that you touched our lives in ways we never thought possible.

Bob and Annie Nash, thank you for coming to our house after we accepted Christ and praying through and anointing our house with oil. Bob, you introduced me to Pastor Dave; we've stayed close from '91 at RLC; and we shared *Experiencing God* by Henry Blackaby. So many good memories.

Pastor Dave, there are too many things to list. Mostly, thank you for always having our backs and always making it about the Scriptures. You invited me to your Tuesday morning men's group, and it was a life changer. You never gave up on us; you took hits on our behalf; you always knew our hearts. Thank you for your humility in how you teach. And Linda, for your friendship and encouragement.

Tuesday morning men's group: the original five men gave me life, vision, and a feeling of place. Watching this group grow and the relationships from it have been incredible.

Kelli Templeton for being an amazing example of what leadership looks like and always believing in our mission for marriages. You were on mission right with us.

Erika Ames for all the work you did to make us look better.

The marriage ministry team at Bethel—it was second to none. We'll always remember Rock Your Marriage when Dave and Ann Wilson walked in on us all praying over the chairs. They said they'd never seen a team like ours anywhere up to that event. Hats off to an amazing team, so many of you.

The Stepping Up leader team started with a few men and grew to over thirty, even while the churches were shut down. You all never stopped. To the core team of seven to ten guys—it felt like we could walk through fire together. You know who you are. Proverbs 27:17 says, "Iron sharpens iron as one man sharpens another," and you men have sharpened me in ways I never thought possible.

All the churches and support couples that have walked alongside us since early 2014 and the over four thousand couples we've served. Nothing happens without you.

The Deer Lake community—from the first coffee time with the men that launched a Wednesday morning men's group to the many marriage classes and several one-day events, then the ten-week Stepping Ups in this small area of only hundreds. Thank you for loving us and accepting us into your community. Lots happened in five-and-a-half years; we think of you often.

To our FamilyLife friends, staff, and support—too many of you to list. We feel supported wherever we are; the encouragement never stops. We appreciate every word you speak over us. From our first Weekend to Remember in 2013 followed by the Love Like You Mean It cruise, we've felt the love and comradery. Yay team! Some of you became our family over the years, and what an amazing family it is.

Dennis and Barbara Rainey—looking back from our very first conversation, we see God had a plan. Thank you for your friendship and love and the constant mentorship. And Dennis, thanks for letting me outshoot you sometimes at pheasant hunting.

Dave and Ann Wilson, we feel blessed to call you friends. We've had so many conversations and so many marriage conferences. We're so glad to be on mission with you.

David and Meg Robbins, what a journey we are all on—thanks for letting us be a part of yours. We for sure feel the support of you being part of ours.

War Room Ministries board, what a journey. We've served together a long time, some of us a decade or so. God doesn't make mistakes; War Room Ministries will go on, and we'll be excited to hear how God works in each and every one of you.

Brian Goins, for getting us started on this project three-and-a-half years ago. You prayed for us, paved the way for us, and supported us through the entire journey. Thanks, Jen, as we know you were also part of this journey.

In memory of Ginger Kolbaba, thank you for starting our book. We know we will see you in heaven and will share how what you started impacted many.

Melodie Turish, thank you for your prayers and direction in finding us our ghostwriter.

Jeannie Deno, for all the great pictures you have taken since 2009. You have a gift. Thanks, Bob, for helping her and for our amazing friendship. You guys were the first couple on our team.

Justin and Falon Unger, from the first time we met at the FamilyLife getaway in DC several years ago at the Museum of the Bible coffee shop—in that original two-and-a-half hours God had a plan for sure. You guys are part of our family. We love you and your four wonderful kids.

To those very special friends who have prayed for, encouraged, served with, and in some cases traveled with us and poured into us, you know who you are. We thank you from the bottom of our hearts. We could not do what we do without your support, commitment, and love!

To Steve and Diana Marlow, for our over three-decade friendship. Steve, for loading my lips to give a gospel conversation with Pop right before he passed. I didn't know what I was doing, but I trusted you that it would be important someday, and it was. Thanks to both of you praying for us and later encouraging us to do iMarriage. You've given us unconditional love and support through all these years, and not just us, but our kids and extended family as well. You are truly family, and we cherish our times together. We love you.

To our kids: Tricia, Jimmy, TJ, Amanda, Blake, and Cara, thanks so much for hanging with us on this journey. We love you all. Thank you especially for granting us forgiveness where we failed.

To our grandkids: James, Trey, Gavin, Shane, Carter, Kaylene, Collins, and Wilder, thank you for the privilege of being your grandparents. We cherish every memory we make together, especially when those memories are driven by Jesus.

Thank you, Liliya Savchuk, for the beautiful Fruit of the Spirit paintings. They will always hang on our walls to enjoy.

Jacob McCall and team, thank you for supporting us to make this book like no other; even though your company is new, you and your team are pros. We can't wait to see the final cuts for the QR videos for this book.

Jonathan Merkh and Forefront staff, thanks for giving us a way to self-publish and have full confidence doing so—maybe even more than if we were with a huge publishing house. You are a pro!

And thanks, Lisa Stilwell—you are so gifted, and we feel so blessed by how you got our voice and shared it in a way that people will understand. You've become a friend and sister in Christ. You've made the journey worth it.

RESOURCES AND RECOMMENDATIONS

If your church, ministry, or other entity is interested in having Tim and Kathy conduct a marriage event, or if you just want to stay connected, go to WarRoomMinistries.com

FamilyLife

Weekend to Remember
Love Like You Mean It Cruise
Art of Marriage
Art of Marriage 2.0
Stepping Up
Art of Parenting
FamilyLife Today Radio

Books

NKJV FamilyLife Marriage Bible
Vertical Marriage: The One Secret That Will Change Your Marriage, by Dave And Ann Wilson; book and study

No Perfect Parents: Ditch Expectations, Embrace Reality, and Discover the One Secret That Will Change Your Parenting, by Dave And Ann Wilson

Love Like You Mean It: The Heart of a Marriage that Honors God, by Bob Lepine; book and study

The Story of Us: A Couples Devotional, by Julia Sullivan

A Lifelong Love: Discovering How Intimacy with God Breathes Passion into Your Marriage, by Gary Thomas

When to Walk Away: Finding Freedom from Toxic People, by Gary Thomas

A Celebration of Sex Guidebook, by Douglas E. Rosenau, Deborah C. Neel, W. Ellen Fox

. . . and all books from the FamilyLife library.

Podcasts

Family Life Today
Married with Benefits (FamilyLife Audio)
The Barbara Rainey Podcast
The Ultimate Intimacy Podcast

Websites

War Room Ministries
WarRoomMinistries.com

Dennis and Barbara Rainey
TheRaineys.org

Ever Thine Home
EverThineHome.com

FamilyLife
FamilyLife.com

FamilyLife Blended Families
FamilyLife.com/blended

Ultimate Intimacy site and app
UltimateIntimacy.com

Married for a Purpose
MarriedForaAPurpose.com

Life Unplugged:
LiveLifeUnplugged.org